THE
SPIRIT OF
THE MOUNTAI.

•TENNESSEANA EDITIONS•

The
Spirit of
the Mountains

by Emma Bell Miles

A FACSIMILE EDITION
WITH A FOREWORD BY
Roger D. Abrahams
AND INTRODUCTION BY
David E. Whisnant

THE UNIVERSITY OF
TENNESSEE PRESS
KNOXVILLE

TENNESSEANA  EDITIONS

Nathalia Wright, General Editor

In the Tennessee Mountains by Mary Noailles Murfree (Charles Egbert Craddock), with an introduction by Nathalia Wright.

William G. Brownlow: Fighting Parson of the Southern Highlands by E. Merton Coulter, with an introduction by James W. Patton.

History of Middle Tennessee; or, Life and Times of Gen. James Robertson by A. W. Putnam, with an introduction by Stanley F. Horn and index by Hugh and Cornelia Walker. Published in cooperation with the Tennessee Historical Commission.

A Narrative of the Life of David Crockett of the State of Tennessee by David Crockett, a facsimile edition with annotations and an introduction by James Atkins Shackford and Stanley J. Folmsbee.

Frontispiece, Emma Bell Miles at work. Mrs. Miles was about thirty-three years old when this photograph was taken by E. A. Wheatley. Photograph courtesy of Mrs. Judith Ford.

Cloth: first printing, 1975; second printing, 1977;
    third printing, 1988.
Paper: first printing, 1985; second printing, 1988;
    third printing, 1994; fourth printing, 2000.

The paper used in this book meets the minimum requirements of ANSI/ NISO Z39.48-1992 (R 1997) (Permanence of Paper). The binding materials have been chosen for strength and durability. Printed on recycled paper.

Library of Congress Cataloging in Publication Data

Miles, Emma Bell, 1879–1919.
        The spirit of the mountains.
        (Tennesseans editions)
        Reprint of the 1905 ed. published by J. Pott, New York.
        Includes index.
        1. Mountain Whites (Southern States)—Social life and customs. 2. Appalachian Mountains, Southern—Social life and customs. I. Title. II. Series.
F217.A65M54   1975   975   75-19222
ISBN 0-87049-181-4 (cloth: alk. paper)
ISBN 0-87049-465-1 (pbk.: alk. paper)

FOREWORD TO THE NEW EDITION

The Spirit of the Mountains is a very special book, particularly for folklorists, and yet it is largely unknown. I did not learn of the book until recently, even though I did my first fieldwork in an area of the Southern Appalachians not unlike that described in this work. Other folklorists apparently are also unfamiliar with the volume, for it is not mentioned in the literature, not even in D. K. Wilgus's encyclopedic *Anglo-American Folksong Scholarship Since 1898* (New Brunswick: Rutgers University Press, 1959). *The Spirit of the Mountains* is an exciting find, all the more, not only because the book is a very early collection of mountain lore (published considerably before Cecil Sharp came to the mountains in 1916), but also because it is written with such great and quiet social insight.

Emma Bell Miles provides us with a sensitive account of the kind of background that folklorists call "context," that is, the social situations in which items of folklore are used. She shows that lore is central to life in the mountains, and tells us why, in terms familiar to the social scientist but at the same time in language that appeals to a much wider audience. This book is an outright plea for understanding but is delivered with directness, simplicity, and conviction.

The Spirit of the Mountains

Virtually every page of *The Spirit of the Mountains* reminds us that folklore does not exist without people, and that traditions persist because they help give order, meaning, and value to a community and its individuals. This perspective at once anticipates the concerns of contemporary folklorists and reminds us of the common-sense sources of our insights. Look for instance at Chapter VI, on the supernatural. It begins with a catalog of what appear to be quaint superstitious practices, peppered with a few playful ones that simply give flavor to life: "If you don't cuss you'll never raise gourds. . . . If you're hairy about the arms and chest you'll have good luck with hogs. . . . If the bread's burnt the cook's mad" (p. 99). The superstitions are almost proverbs—they deal with social style as much as with natural or supernatural occurrence. But as soon as the reader is caught up with the playful approach, Aunt Neppie Ann is introduced. The reader is then shown, by Aunt Neppie's stories, that such beliefs are important to the way individuals live in a real (and often hostile) environment and how they talk about their lives. We are given many "texts" of superstitions, but more important we are given the stories by which these beliefs are validated. Aunt Neppie comes to life not because she is superstitious, but because her "fine old stories" demonstrate how beliefs have explained and given order to people's lives in the past. But Mrs. Miles gives us much more than just the superstition, story, or song: Aunt Neppie and her family discuss and challenge some of these very beliefs.

Mrs. Miles's observations on performance style are especially valuable. Simply juxtaposing religious and secular songs and their singing styles, and then asking "why," is an analytic technique that folklorists are only now learning how to employ—yet this is precisely the method of the fine chapter on songs, "Some Real American Music." Without a great deal of to-do, we find ourselves presented with the religious singing style of rocking to and fro and sudden leaping and shouting and pitching about, and we are asked to relate this to the setting of a brush-arbor or a "half-lighted log church . . . reinforced by the vibrant, hurried voices of exhorters and the high strained sing-song of the preacher who has reached what is known as his 'weavin' way' " (p. 154). How important, we may now ask, is the connection between this and the secular rocking style of singing in the homes, and the "weavin' way" of the hard drinker and sinner? These questions are not answered, but the fact that they can be posed seems significant. Would that Cecil Sharp and his genteel followers had given us as much detail from their observations or had had such a sense of the totality and integrity of the singing repertoire.

But I do not want to seem to be claiming too much for this little book. It is hardly an unusual kind of book, only an especially perceptive example of a genre. It reveals a way of life in an area much drawn upon and discussed by folklorists, but never so fully and richly rendered. Mrs. Miles, anticipating many of the social concerns of the third generation of the twentieth century, lectures us, gently and often wistfully, about the integrity of life in a mountain community. Conspicuously absent is any great attempt to make us feel guilty; rather, we witness a proud person giving testimony to the positive, if harsh, qualities of daily existence in the mountains.

Her characters are real, but we never get to know them very well, for their interactions exhibit a kind of deep inner privacy that reflects what many others have found in the mountains—a sense of friendship and respect for others, but a strong tendency to express emotions obliquely, often somewhat impersonally. Coming from a culture in which feelings are valued most when rendered directly and at highest pitch, one may be pleasantly surprised to witness such an art of indirection drawing on the voices of tradition for personal effect. Not only the songs, which speak about people's feelings mostly through action or highly conventional images, but also the day-to-day relationships of the mountain people reflect this indirection. Repeatedly I have heard a pathetic song or a story performed by a mountaineer in a purely descriptive narrative style, only to find out later that someone in the family of the performer had actually been involved in the imparted event, even been the victim of the crime or disaster. Emotions are veiled, but not because of psychological repression or sublimation; rather, deeply felt sentiments are presented in a nonpersonal, acceptable style. One may thus make a personal statement without appearing to be out of the ordinary, for it implies a recognition of the common aspects of the human condition. We do not, I suppose, like to be told that our problems are common ones, but there is solace in such perceptions in communities like Walden's Ridge. In a fascinating way, Mrs. Miles's manner of describing the people and their lives reflects the restraint of the community's styles. Her voice is that of an observer, engaged yet generally objective, aware of attitudes both within the community and outside of it.

The Spirit of the Mountains is, then, a splendid example of that special kind of travel book in which life in a culturally different (and usually backwater) area is reported from an essentially bucolic point of view. The reader is presumed to be an urbanite nostalgic for what he imagines his agrarian past must have been like and, thus, sympathetic to those who continue to live simply in an essentially homogeneous community. Our American version of pastoral has frequently looked toward the south, if not always to the Southern Mountains. It is an agrarian vision that has been detailed by travelers from William Byrd and James Agee to Robert Coles. It has become an increasingly complex mode, for all of the problems of a class structure, overlaid with apprehensions of cultural as well as moral decadence, intrude in such accounts. Though this complexity has not been very evident in accounts of Appalachian life, the literature from writers such as Kephart, Arnow, and Caudill has increasingly been concerned with those forces (predominantly from the technological national culture) which have brought the Machine into the Garden.

This kind of nostalgia is by its very nature ambivalent. On the one hand, the sophisticate is drawn to the country because of its promise of restored harmony of self and society with nature, and through this a restoration of innocence. On the other, there is always fear of the lack of morality and order that lies behind the loss of civility. Thus, in the eyes of outsiders, the mountaineer becomes the decadent, ignorant, incestuous hillbilly.

Books such as *The Spirit of the Mountains* are commonly written by apostles of civilization, but by apostles who because of their moral persuasion see these culturally different people as representatives of an equally viable heritage. The writers habitually betray the perspective of a missionary who comes into a strange world to tell of the new while helping to maintain the old. This was also the spirit of the abolitionists going south, establishing schools and churches for the ignorant ones they found there. These travel books are tinged with a kind of low-profile drama bespeaking what good works have been done—and what amusing cross-cultural mistakes are made in the process. Further, we learn how the visitor comes to be loved by the visited in spite of misunderstandings. We have had aplenty our Annas among the Siamese (I think of the parade of them in the Sea Islands, from Botume and Higginson to Lydia Parrish and the Carawans, not to mention the Campbells and Jean Thomas in the mountains).

Inevitably we learn a great deal about people of other cultures from such books, for they do dwell on the experiences by which we all become socialized and acculturated. Consequently, we are frequently given descriptions of the "daily life of the inhabitants," the obligatory chapters which in older travel books are called "manners and customs of the natives." The idea, of course, is to make the indigenes seem human. But such descriptions are colored with the cultural background of the people doing the describing, especially because the accounts are addressed to readers who share their models of perception. Moreover, it is difficult for a writer to retreat from the cute or the sensational approach; only the very best writers are able to resist—not by giving up stereotyping, but by making it clear just what the images and presuppositions are. The anthropologist writing an ethnography is confronted with the same problem, of course, and often chooses to mask his own cultural presumptions behind an objective writing persona. He can analyze a particular culture and convey information systematically without rendering much real behavior as behavior. A simple analysis is not an option open to the local-color travel writer, however, for the reader of such writing is looking for real behavior described through personal experience. And this approach perforce invokes the stereotype of the culturally different.

Emma Bell Miles knew of this stereotype, had obviously encountered it as a mountain person living in the city; she was not averse to drawing on it herself in this work. Although she did not hesitate to speak out on the harshness of life in the mountains, even this was colored by a Thoreauvian persuasion that a hard life is honest and redemptive. Even if, through both her word-pictures and illustrations, she does paint mountain existence in pastoral hues, her interpretation never arises from any vision of innocence and simplicity in mountain life, but from experiences of the wholeness of the fabric of life there and the unthinking ease by which it is rent with the introduction of city products and ways.

In *The Spirit of the Mountains,* mountain people are sometimes "we," but much more often "they." It is as if, in 1905, the outsider's travel account were the only medium open to a woman who wished to describe, however sympathetically, a culture outside the mainstream. So closely does Mrs. Miles adhere to the conventions of the genre that, before I learned the details of her life, I assumed that she had come to the community as an outsider, a school teacher bringing enlightenment to the "simple" folk (an epithet which she employs). Nor does she allay that presumption; to the contrary, she plays upon the reader's expectations by using her role as teacher to show how mountain children live in harmony with nature, even while going to school.

Although there is a firm depiction of economic poverty in this book, the author hardly makes any pitch for public assistance. Rather, this bare subsistence pattern of life is depicted as suffused with "the charm of pioneer hardihood, of primitive peace, of the fatalism of ancient peoples . . . " (p. 18). But once beyond this pastoral litany, we are given an informed and amazingly detailed depiction of the folklife of mountain people. In brief glimpses we discover a great many factors of this environment that lead to crucial life choices: where the cabin should be placed and why, what it is made of and how, what the major canons of cleanliness are for both the cabin and the household, what chores and pleasant moments make up a day at the cabin. Emma Bell Miles is particularly perceptive on the importance of women, especially older women, in the preservation of mountain life-ways—her perceptions arising, as her diaries and accounts of her acquaintances show, from her own painful experiences of trying to raise a family and maintain a difficult marriage in the most austere of conditions.

Little of this personal agony shows through in *The Spirit of the Mountains,* and never in despairing tones. To the contrary, it is a sunny book and a great "find," one which will be greeted by the very many who are interested in mountain life, in the old ways, and especially in a mode of life in which doing for oneself is the basic requirement of existence.

ROGER D. ABRAHAMS

Turkeyfoot, Texas
March 1975

CONTENTS

INTRODUCTION TO THE NEW EDITION

> This locality has three special characteristics
> which . . . are perhaps not to be duplicated in all
> the world. They are silence, blue air, and an end-
> less variety.
>
> *Journal of Emma Bell Miles*
> *November 29, 1908*

The Spirit of the Mountains is one of the few books about Appalachia and its people which neither romanticizes nor condescends, and which does not depend for its analysis upon the unconscious acceptance of middle-class, mainstream American values. Relatively unnoticed when it was published in October 1905 (I found no record of a review), and read by few during the ensuing three-quarters of a century, it has acquired a fresh and compelling relevance as the problems of Appalachia have been thrust again to the foreground during the past decade.

In this new edition, *The Spirit of the Mountains* should speak to an audience both different from and broader than the one it had in its own time. Throughout the mountains, individuals and groups are seeking to halt the destruction of their lands and homes by stripmining, new highways, and dams; to build schools that serve their needs and sustain their values; to preserve alternative ways of life instead of passively merging with the mainstream; to find meaningful work. Their efforts are frequently viewed as a model by other minority groups beyond the mountains, who are also resisting the pressures of economic exploitation and cultural assimilation. Concurrently, a growing number of scholars and writers are outlining a new social, political, and economic history not only of Appalachia but of most other exploited minorities. *The Spirit of the Mountains* has much to offer such a diverse audience.

I had heard of *The Spirit of the Mountains* several years before I read it. For most of the sixty or so years following its publication, it apparently has been known only to a few historians and literary scholars, such as West Virginia University's Robert F. Munn, who wrote of it briefly in *Mountain Life and Work* in 1965. At the very end of the 1960s, the book began to be referred to among a few political activists as an early call for Appalachian nationalism written by a *bona fide* "insider," a forgotten but welcome antidote to the many condescending books by "outsiders." It gained further recognition when one chapter was printed in Irmgard Best's *Appalachians Speak Up* (1972).

But *The Spirit of the Mountains* is not a tract, and Emma Bell Miles was not a single-minded, native-born political partisan. Reading closely, one is struck by her profound biculturism and her only subtly implicit politics. She was a keen observer of the complex interplay between mountain people's lives and life elsewhere, and the book's politics arise quite naturally and organically from her close attention to that interaction. She knew that every summer tourist who came to the mountains, every mountain boy or girl who chose a mate from town was both responding to and affecting a profoundly important political and cultural dynamic. Indeed she herself was part of that dynamic.

It was Emma Bell Miles's fate (and good fortune) to live between two cultures. Her life lay primarily among the mountain people on Walden's Ridge, but for two decades her work as a writer and painter involved her intimately with the wealthy society people of Chattanooga. Her feelings about both can only be called intensely ambivalent. Her intelligence, integrity, and honesty made her acutely (even painfully) conscious of the strengths and weaknesses, coherence and contradictions of the lives of both mountain people and those from the city who were steadily buying their land for summer homes and then offering them jobs as maids and gardeners. Thus the central fact of Emma Bell Miles's life and the predominant theme of her book is ambivalence and biculturism.

Emma Bell Miles was born October 19, 1879, in Evansville, Indiana, to B. T. and Martha Ann (Mirick) Bell. A twin brother Elmer lived only one day, and Emma herself never enjoyed robust health. The family moved a year or so later to Rabbit Hash, Kentucky, just across the river from Cincinnati, where her parents taught school. When she was about nine years old, the family moved to the small community of Red Bank, at the foot of Walden's Ridge near Chattanooga. About 1891, Mr. Bell bought land and built a two-story frame house at the top of the tortuously crooked W-Road that led to the summit of the ridge. There Emma Bell spent her adolescent years.[1]

Emma Bell's formal education was spotty because she was

[1]Reliable biographical information on Emma Bell Miles is not plentiful. Details used here are taken from telephone interviews with her daughters Judith Miles Ford and Jean Miles Catino, from her manuscript journal (1908–1917), from a few letters in the Chattanooga Public Library, and from a few other scattered sources. Adelaide Rowell's "Emma Bell Miles: Artist, Author and Poet of the Tennessee Mountains," *Tennessee Historical Quarterly* 25 (Spring 1966), 77–89, and Abby Crawford Milton's introduction to *Strains from a Dulcimore* (Atlanta: Bozart Press, 1930) both contain serious errors of fact and must be used with caution.

kept out of school by frequent illness. Her later statement that she was "educated on *Harper's Magazine*" was only partially true; she was a voracious reader who had read *Pilgrim's Progress* and Hawthorne's *The Marble Faun* by the age of eight. "I drew, read, wrote a little," she said of her early life on the Ridge, "and lived with the mountain people and in the woods a great deal."[2] At about the age of sixteen, she saved a dollar and walked to call on an art teacher, whom she asked for "a dollar's worth" of lessons.[3] The long, solitary afternoons she spent intently studying art reproductions in T. H. Payne's department store in Chattanooga drew the attention of some wealthy patrons who arranged for her to study for two years in St. Louis.[4]

The St. Louis sojourn could have been the beginning of a permanent exile from the mountains, and an entrance to the genteel world of *Harper's Magazine*. "[But] I felt that I had no part in the life about me in St. Louis," Emma Bell wrote to Anna Ricketson later. "[It] was like a world of dreams; I wanted to go back to the mountains and reality . . . . That summer I spent in the woods, trying to 'find myself' . . . . I was married in the fall of that year."

On October 30, 1901, Emma Bell married G. Frank Miles, to whom she had been engaged for more than two years. Miles was descended from one of the first two mountain

[2]Letter to Anna Ricketson, April 6, 1907; Chattanooga Public Library. Anna Ricketson was drama and music critic for the New Bedford (Mass.) *Standard-Times* and *Mercury* for several decades before her death in 1949. See *New York Times,* June 17, 1949, p. 24.

[3]Rowell, "Emma Bell Miles," 79.

[4]Adelaide Rowell and others have reported (in the Chattanooga *Times,* Jan. 1933) that some of Emma Bell's drawings and paintings were exhibited at the St. Louis Exposition. They may indeed have been, but none are listed in the *Official Catalog of Exhibitors: Universal Exposition, St. Louis, U. S. A., 1904* (St. Louis, 1904). Several published sources say friends from Chattanooga paid for the schooling, but an Emma Bell Miles letter of April 6, 1907, states that "some wealthy St. Louis friends" paid.

families to settle on Walden's Ridge before the Civil War.[5] When she met him, he was driving the public hack that ran from Chattanooga to the top of the Ridge. Her parents opposed the marriage (there are letter and journal references to being "disowned"), and she herself feared the reactions of her wealthy benefactors who had paid for her schooling in St. Louis. "I've been afraid to tell anyone I was married," she confided in a letter. "[I] got so many scoldings. [But I] just laid low until I had a big portfolio of work to show for answer."[6] Despite the disapproval of parents and friends, however, it is clear from Emma Bell Miles's journal that Frank Miles was not only sensitive and intelligent (they spent long afternoons tramping through the woods and reading Thoreau aloud to each other), but that he embodied for her the authentic and concrete reality of mountain people and their culture, to which she returned to find herself after the alienation of St. Louis. "He is a touchstone," she wrote in her journal years after her marriage. "All things are tested as rung against the perfect sincerity of his nature."[7]

And yet the disapproval voiced by those who (as she later recalled it) felt that "I had thrown my life away" was not wholly unreasonable. Her life with Frank Miles turned out to be extraordinarily difficult. His health was poor, and he was chronically impractical about money; work was irregular and the family was continually in debt. She served, as she said in bitterness years later, a "life sentence at hard labor" with Miles: wind through the cracks in the floors of a series of rented cabins, sickness, bad food (or no food), miscarriages, the needless death of a child, and bundles of used clothing to be made over for herself and four children.[8]

[5]Cartter Patten, *Signal Mountain and Walden's Ridge* (Chattanooga: [the author], 1962), 16–17.
[6]Letter to Mr. and Mrs. Donnell, Jan. 1902; courtesy of Judith Miles Ford.
[7]Journal, Feb. 28, 1912.
[8]Journal, April 28, 1915. The journal contains innumerable references to

Emma Bell's life with Frank Miles dramatized above all the insoluble and tortured dividedness of her biculturism. She could write bitterly of his relatives as a "lewd and drunken crew"; speak in disgust of his "cruel sensuality"; lament his lack of manners and collars; wish he would "learn daintier ways" with handkerchiefs, toothbrushes, and underclothing; and flee from his "tobacco spit and stale perspiration."[9] When she hated him and all he represented, she referred to him as "Frank"; when she loved him she called him—after the manner of mountain women—"my man," spoke of his "moral elegance," and saw in him what she considered to be beautiful and mythic qualities of the lives of mountaineers:

> They are all romance, these luxuries of the mountaineer,—music, whiskey, firelight, religion, and fighting; they are efforts to reach a finer, larger life, —part of the blue dream of the wild land. Who knows him? Who has ever understood the devious approaches of his mind to any subject? Who has tracked him to that wild, remote spot, echo-haunted, beautiful, terrible, where he dwells? Who has measured the rock foundation of his home, or tasted the water of his unknown well-springs of desire?[10]

The hatred she sometimes felt for Frank Miles was also tempered by the knowledge that his own life—and the lives of most mountain people—had been scarred by pain and want. "Frank has been telling me tales of his boyhood," she wrote in her journal during the summer of 1912,

> of the murder of John Pickett the moonshiner, not twenty minutes after the boy and his father had

---

lack of money, food, clothing, and other essentials. There were five children: twins Jean and Judith (b. 1902); Joe (b. 1905); Katherine (b. 1907); and Mirick (b. 1909), who died before reaching maturity.

[9]Journal, May 26, 1914.

[10]Journal, Sept. 7 and 10, 1913; Nov. 13, 1908.

left him on Market Street; of whole nights spent in a barroom, watching his drunken father play cards, sleeping on a table and subsisting on what sandwiches and soft drinks the bartender gave him; of a runaway on the [mountain] in the dark, when he, all alone at twelve years, guided the team home through the burning woods; of his early acquaintance with all the vice in the lowest dives in Chattanooga.[11]

Emma Bell Miles's life was lived mainly with her husband and his people, but she was also an intellectual, an artist, and a writer whose need for an audience, a market, and personal support drew her into the lives of quite a different set of people. For years she was the darling of the wealthy and socially prominent of Chattanooga. They displayed her paintings and illustrated books in their homes, paid her to paint murals on the walls of their drawing rooms,[12] lamented what they considered the bad judgment that led her to marry a mountain man from Walden's Ridge, and sheltered her as she made her way back and forth between the intellectually and emotionally impoverished drudgery of life in a tumble-down cabin on the ridge, and the solitary comfort of private homes or spartan rented rooms in town, where she could paint and write and attend concerts and lectures.

Her professional career therefore, like her personal life, was infused with painful ambivalence toward both of the cultures of which she was a part. From the time she published her first poem in 1904, through the writing and publication of *The Spirit of the Mountains* in 1905, to her last work fifteen years later, she felt both immersed in a traditional culture of extraordinary and unexamined richness, and isolated from what

[11]Journal, June 20, 1912.
[12]In a letter to Anna Ricketson of Oct. 24, 1907, she told of working three weeks to decorate a parlor in the city and of receiving seven dollars for her labor.

she at times saw as the "real" culture of the metropolitan northeast.

She knew, valued, and wrote extensively about the culture of mountain people: their music, dances, legends, and folkways. She resented the pressures that were being exerted upon it, speaking at one point in *The Spirit of the Mountains* of a pathetic "home missionary of culture" who came from beyond the mountains to teach in a local one-room school. But the world beyond the mountains she herself also longed for. It too offered things her spirit needed, and its nearest palpable representative was the pretentious social posturing of her city friends: their elegant parlors and chamber orchestras, wine and flowers, carriages, and books.

And yet those people who offered her hemstitched sheets to sleep on now and then were the same ones who were exploiting her as an artist and writer, and she knew it. For nearly twenty years she tried to support herself and her family by painting what she once called "these wretched little daubs of souvenirs"—miniature landscapes, place cards, post cards—anything that would sell to tourists, summer people, and people in town. She hated being forced to prostitute her talents, but could find no alternative. On a rainy day in June 1912, she noted in her journal that she had painted "fourteen of those confounded . . . little landscapes." The summer people she found "hopelessly bound by their class philosophy and bourgeois ideals, with the cramp of their own psychology ineradicable in their minds."[13]

Emma Bell Miles made a persistent effort both to mediate the ambivalences that were inescapable in her own life, and to stay in touch with a world beyond, which, when all was said and done, she needed to keep some parts of her mind and spirit alive. After she published a poem in the *Century* in

[13]Journal, Jan. 7 and 10, 1912.

1906, she received a letter from New England drama and music critic Anna Ricketson. Her reply revealed her acute sense of isolation:

> It meant so much to me to receive a message right out of the heart of that land of literary traditions and great names, from one so intimately connected with both. You know it is quite different here in the mountains, where the traditions, while of deep import and interest and capable of giving rise to a literature are, so far, anything but literary. . . . I know of no one who reads Thoreau except my husband. We discovered him ourselves quite by accident.[14]

For ten years she corresponded regularly with Anna Ricketson, and read as much as she could manage. An early letter (and many journal entries) refer to her reading of Ibsen, Shakespeare, Thoreau, and others.[15] A well-marked copy of Tolstoy's *Resurrection* survives among her papers.

Ultimately, however, the ambivalence could not be resolved nor the isolation relieved. The boxes of clothing, books, and art supplies that arrived occasionally from Anna Ricketson and her literary friends only underscored that fact. After 1912, when the last of Emma Bell Miles's stories had appeared in *Harper's, Lippincott's,* and *Putnam's,* she apparently wrote little except a series of signed columns ("Fountain Square Conversations") in the Chattanooga *News* during the summer of 1914.[16]

After 1912 Emma Bell Miles's life became more difficult

[14]Letter of Feb. 20, 1907; Chattanooga Public Library.
[15]Letter to Mr. and Mrs. Donnell, Jan. 13, 1902.
[16]The *News* columns (especially those for the latter half of May) reveal her strong interest in the women's suffrage movement, opposition to the U. S. military expedition against Pancho Villa, and reform movements elsewhere in the country. Her journal for this period contains some oblique references to "my novel" and perhaps other writings, but so far none have come to light except a long philosophical essay entitled "The Good Gray Mother" in the possession of Jean Miles Catino.

and unsettled than ever. Her painful relationship with Frank Miles kept her in an almost continual series of separations and reconciliations—moving each time between rented rooms in the city and a cabin on the mountain. During the fall of 1913, Frank was on Walden's Ridge, the older daughters had been sent to school in Alabama, and Emma Bell and the two other children were living in one room on Georgia Avenue in Chattanooga. At other times she boarded for $3.50 a week at the home for working girls. In her journal for May 20, 1913, she noted, "I have used my last stretcher of canvas." During the winter of 1916, when the family was living in a tarpaper shack, she wrote to Anna Ricketson, "I have papered the main room with two coats of newspapers, adding greatly to its comfort, light, and cleanliness."[17]

In May 1916, diagnosis confirmed symptoms of tuberculosis that had been present for years, and Emma Bell Miles was sent to Pine Breeze Sanitarium. Such treatments as were then popular (e.g., requiring patients to sleep in unheated tents year-round) probably hastened her death, which occurred on May 20, 1919, in a small house at 110 Lawn Street in north Chattanooga. Her book *Our Southern Birds*, for which she had continued to paint illustrations until shortly before her death, was published posthumously.

The Spirit of the Mountains

Most books about the mountains, quite unlike this book by Emma Bell Miles, have been written by those who came, observed, and left to resume their own comfortable and conventional lives elsewhere. So relatively uncomplicated is the process, in fact, that such books have been in rather abundant supply since the eighteenth century, when European travelers began to penetrate the Appalachian region and record their

[17]Letter of Feb. 17, 1916; Chattanooga Public Library.

observations. One of the earliest accounts was written by a British spy, J. F. D. Smyth, who published a narrative of his mission in the Carolinas and Virginia in 1784.[18] Although mountain people had been a subject of random curiosity and condescension since William Byrd's celebrated comments in *The History of the Dividing Line* (1729), George Tucker's *The Valley of the Shenandoah* (1824) was perhaps the first book to propose that mountaineers constituted a distinct group. By the time of the Civil War, mountaineers had emerged as a recognizable literary type. Although the tradition of travelers' accounts continued into the 1880s with such books as Wilbur Ziegler and Ben S. Grosscup's *The Heart of the Alleghanies* (1883) and Charles Dudley Warner's *On Horseback: a Tour of Virginia, North Carolina and Tennessee* (1889), fiction and "in depth" studies came to predominate.

Fiction took the form of literally hundreds of stories published in genteel magazines by such writers as Joel Chandler Harris and Rebecca Harding Davis, and of scores of novels by Mary Noailles Murfree (whose *The Prophet of the Great Smoky Mountains* of 1885 Cratis Williams has called the first American novel to concentrate primarily on mountain people), John Fox, Jr. (*The Little Shepherd of Kingdom Come* [1903]; *The Trail of the Lonesome Pine* [1908]), Lucy Furman, Maristan Chapman, Will N. Harben, and later writers such as Jesse Stuart, James Still, and Harriette Arnow.

The "in depth" studies, while less numerous than the novels and stories, have formed just as persistent a strain. They began in earnest around the turn of the century, when mountain people had come to be called "our southern highlanders,"

[18] J. F. D. Smyth, *A Tour of the United States of America* (Dublin, 1784). Cited in Cratis D. Williams, "The Southern Mountaineer in Fact and Fiction," (Diss., New York Univ., 1961), 181. Portions of the following section are based upon Williams. For a survey of early travelers' accounts, see Lawrence S. Thompson, "From Elvas to Chattanooga: Three Centuries of Travel in Appalachia," *Appalachian Notes* 1 (Second Quarter, 1973), 1–11.

"our contemporary ancestors," or (in a phrase that stuck for more than a half-century) "yesterday's people."[19] Such studies range from the näive *The Carolina Mountains* (1913) by Margaret Morley to Horace Kephart's more reliable *Our Southern Highlanders* of the same year. The next decade produced James Watt Raine's *The Land of Saddlebags* (1924) and John C. Campbell's classic *The Southern Highlander and His Homeland* (1921). Studies of mountain people have shown no recent signs of abating. Thomas R. Ford's *The Southern Appalachian Region: a Survey* (1962) was produced by a quarter-million dollar grant from the Ford Foundation. The "community studies" undertaken by Mandel Sherman and Thomas R. Henry (*Hollow Folk* [1933]), Marion Pearsall (1959), John B. Stephenson (1968), and others continue at their best in John Fetterman's *Stinking Creek* (1970) and at their worst in Rena Gazaway's *The Longest Mile* (1969).

Most observers of complex realities see more or less what they expect to see, and thus it has been with the mountains and mountaineers. To some they have been the depraved and inbred upland cousins of the crackers—comical and worthless hillbillies; to others they have been the quaint and picturesque preservers of the best of our Elizabethan and native heritage, singing ballad after ancient ballad to an astonished Cecil Sharp and enlisting in droves for every war; to others they have been an "analgesic subculture" upon whose poverty and supposed cultural deprivation several unsuccessful wars have been declared.[20]

The Spirit of the Mountains is not entirely free of the faults

[19]See William G. Frost, "Our Contemporary Ancestors in the Southern Mountains," *Atlantic Monthly* 83 (March 1899), 311–19; Horace Kephart, *Our Southern Highlanders* (New York: Outing Publishers, 1913); and Jack Weller, *Yesterday's People: Life in Contemporary Appalachia* (Lexington: Univ. of Kentucky Press, 1965).

[20]See for example Ellen Churchill Semple, "The Anglo-Saxons of the Kentucky Mountains; a Study in Anthropogeography," *Geographical Journal* 17 (1901), 588–623; and Richard Ball, "A Poverty Case: the Analgesic Subcul-

that mar so many other books about the mountains, but Emma Bell Miles wrote as nearly perfectly as she did because she had two advantages lacked by many another writer: a superb native intelligence that lent rare insight and subtlety to her analysis, and a consciously dual perspective on her own life and those of mountain people that gave her writing a generous scope and fine balance. The stock in trade of most writing about the mountains is the normative cultural judgment, but *The Spirit of the Mountains* turns upon irony, paradox, and the necessarily relativistic nature of all cultural judgments.

The Spirit of the Mountains was written while Emma Bell Miles was teaching at the old Log Church School on Walden's Ridge during the years immediately following her marriage. It was published late in the fall of 1905, and was illustrated with her own paintings of mountain scenes and characters.

In its opening pages, *The Spirit of the Mountains* conveys the richness and vitality of mountain life. If the pupils at the Log Church School are ignorant (as that benighted state is conventionally defined), they are nevertheless veritable mines of ancient and valuable lore, legends, and tales. Hence "If the young minds wander afield . . . what matter? Perhaps they learn . . . something not to be found between the covers of Webster" (p. 5). "Every phase of the mountaineer's life," she says later, "connects in some way with tradition anciently received" (p. 98).

Although she admits that in some respects the existence of mountain people is "nearly as primitive as the Dark Ages," she sees them as victims of social and political inequities. She dispenses quickly with the conventional notion that mountain people are innately degenerate and lawless: "There is certainly a class of mountain people, dirty, degenerate, incred-

ture of the Southern Appalachians," *American Sociological Review* 33 (Dec. 1968), 885–95.

ibly ignorant and unintelligent, very little superior to savages. It exists, but I have lived in many different localities in the Kentucky and Tennessee mountains and have never seen it yet" (pp. 75–76). On lawlessness she says simply: "How different from the actual state of affairs is that widespread popular idea, fostered by newspaper stories, that no class of people in America is more lawless than the mountaineers" (p. 74). Her position on these and related matters, grounded in both common sense and acute observation, was that negative personal and social traits occurred in the mountains with about the same frequency that they occurred elsewhere.

Life in the mountains seemed as rich, varied, and complex to Emma Bell Miles as life anywhere else.[21] "Only a superficial observer could fail to understand that the mountain people really love their wilderness," she said, "love it for its beauty, for its freedom":

> I once rode up the [mountain] with a grandmother from Sawyers' Springs, who cried out, as the overhanging curve of the bluff, crowned with pines, came into view: "Now, ain't that finer than any picter you ever seed in your life?—and they call us pore mountaineers! . . ."
> Nothing less than the charm of their stern motherland could hold them here. . . . Occasionally a whole starved-out family will emigrate westward, and, having settled, will spend years in simply waiting for a chance to sell out and move back again. All alike cling to the ungracious acres they have so patiently and hardly won, because of the wild world that lies outside their puny fences, because of the dream-vistas, blue and violet, that lead their eyes afar among the hills. . . . (pp. 18–19)

[21]It is important to understand that her own personal longing for the culture beyond the mountains stemmed from the perception that it was *different* (and therefore capable of serving different needs), not that it was superior in any absolute sense.

Comparing mountain people with their wealthier and supposedly more refined neighbors in town, she observed that "the mountaineer takes the same pride in his water supply as the rich man in his wine cellar, and is in this respect a connoisseur" (p. 19). Her description of a typical day in a mountain cabin shows people's lives—despite the hardships and the aberrations of behavior produced by unremitting want—to be ordered, gentle, purposeful, abundant in feeling, and generous in hospitality and in a spirit of gift-giving (pp. 25–34, 80–81).

Emma Bell Miles was at her best, however, in discussing the relationships between men and women in the mountains, and the effects of economic change upon mountain culture and society. "A rift is set between the sexes at babyhood," she observed, and it "widens with the passing of the years." People are "robbed of life's sweetest gift by the continual failure of well-meant efforts to bridge the gulf fixed by the mountaineers between woman and man." Young people meet "almost as formally as young Japanese," and when they are married—as she shows in her extended portrait of the marriage of Gideon and Mary Burns (pp. 40–70)—the gulf is not closed "even by the daily interdependence of a poor man's partnership with his wife. . . . They are so silent. They know so pathetically little of each other's lives" (pp. 64–70).

She sees much of the strength and endurance of mountain life as residing in and depending upon the older women, whom she calls "old prophetesses . . . repositories of tribal lore—tradition and song, medical and religious learning. They are the nurses, the teachers of practical arts, the priestesses" (p. 37). A mountain woman, she says, "belongs to the race, to the *old people*," while a man represents the "high daring and merciless recklessness of youth and the characteristic grim humor of the American" (pp. 68–69). Men dominate the day-to-day superficial functioning of mountain society, but women sustain at the level of knowing, coping, creating, and providing continuity generation to generation. The portrait of the ancient Aunt Geneva Rogers (pp. 37ff.) is impressive in its depth and richness, almost epic in its proportions:

> there is something terrible about old Geneva Rogers, a fascination, as of the stern and awful patience of some grand, stubborn slave. At an age when the mothers of any but a wolf-race become lace-capped and felt-shod pets of the household . . . she is yet able to toil almost as severely as ever. . . . Her strength and endurance are beyond imagination to women of the sheltered life. (p. 54)

One crucial determinant of the relations between women and men in the mountains, as Emma Bell Miles well knew from her own life, was the social and cultural disruption attendant upon economic change. Even in 1905, the impact of economic and commercial development and exploitation was being felt on Walden's Ridge, which mercifully lacked the coal seams of the nearby Sequatchie Valley, but whose forests and cool air were attracting growing numbers of tourists and summer residents from the growing industrial center of Chattanooga.

Emma Bell Miles's intimate awareness of the delicately interdependent cultural and social ecology of mountain life, and the threats to it posed by what is now called "regional development," is fully revealed in her comments on the music, oral literature, religion, lore and legends of mountain people (see Roger Abrahams' analysis preceding this Introduction). In addition, however, the entire final chapter of *The Spirit of the Mountains* elaborates a central assumption about the effects of development. "My people," she says, "are being laid hold of and swept away by the oncoming tide of civilization, that drowns as many as it uplifts" (p. 190). A factory, a mill, a summer hotel "presents the thin edge of the wedge . . . [and] a host of evils follow" (p. 191).

As the twentieth century opened, Walden's Ridge was rapidly being turned into a haven of summer hotels and second homes for the wealthy who bought the land at bargain rates and hired the displaced mountain people as maids, janitors, caretakers, stable boys, and gardeners. They were "growing old in a service which provides no pension" (p. 194). She said:

> Too late the mountaineer realizes that he has sold his birthright for a mess of pottage. He has become a day laborer, with nothing better in store, and can give his sons no heritage but the prospect of working by the day. . . . the semblance of prosperity is only a temporary illusion that vanishes with the departure of the summer people. (pp. 195–96)[22]

In the process, farms are lost, traditions and survival skills fall into disuse, and self-hatred follows as mountain people are "brought under the yoke of caste division" (p. 198), reduced to picking blackberries for the summer people.

The pattern was not new, of course, when Emma Bell Miles commented upon it, nor has it disappeared in the intervening seventy years. As early as 1860, Frederick Law Olmsted, in *A Journey to the Back Country*, reported seeing mountain women picking blackberries to sell to resort visitors northeast of Asheville.[23] More than a century later, the Appalachian Regional Commission's federal-state highway building program includes the construction of Corridor K (Chattanooga to Asheville), one of whose explicit purposes is to encourage

[22]Her story "Three Roads and a River," *Harper's Monthly* 121 (Nov. 1910), 882–89, is about the devastating effects upon a mountain family after the government built a road at Hutson's Ferry: the family's ferry business dies, their farm is lost, and the father in despair ultimately attempts to poison his wife and children. "Broken Urn," *Putnam's* 5 (Feb. 1909), 574–80, also contains elements of the same theme.

[23]See Cratis Williams, "The Southern Mountaineer," 246.

tourist development. The commission has also established "hospitality training" programs (in Asheville and in Nelsonville, Ohio) to prepare mountain young people for "careers" as maids, janitors, and waitresses in the tourism industry, which now as in 1905 offers only low-skill, low-wage, nonunion, seasonal jobs.

Thus portions of *The Spirit of the Mountains,* as it now becomes available to another generation of readers, will speak strongly to those who are concerned with major cultural and economic issues in the region: poverty, exploitation by developers and entrepreneurs, retention of cultural identity, reclamation of ravaged land, and restoration of control of institutions. It should also speak to those who make policy for the region, and to those whose business it is to ponder and write about the dynamics of cultural interaction in a pluralistic society. Its portrait of the strengths (and its admission of the weaknesses) of mountain life should have a fresh appeal to mountain young people who in an age of mass communications and myopic regional development must face their own inevitable biculturism and try to understand for themselves the spirit of the mountains.

The conclusion of *The Spirit of the Mountains* is deeply grounded in Emma Bell Miles's own bicultural experience:

> In the mountains the need is for development not foreign to our natures. . . . Let us be given work that will make us better mountaineers, instead of turning us into poor imitation city people. . . . [Mountaineers] will yet become a grand race; a race that shall stand for freedom political and industrial; a race that can no more endure unjust rule than it can thrive in the tainted air of the low country. . . .
>
> But before such renaissance the mountaineers must awaken to consciousness of themselves as a people. . . . [We] are yet a people asleep . . . with-

out knowledge of [our] own existence. (pp. 198–201)

When Robert F. Munn quoted this passage in 1965, he judged it to betoken "an extreme type of Appalachian nationalism" which assumed that "improvement was to come from within due to an awareness of a collective reality as a superior people."[24] But such a judgment overlooks the book's essentially bicultural point of view, which tempers all judgments of mountain people with an awareness of the interdependence of complementary types in a pluralistic culture. Instead of asserting the absolute superiority of mountain people, Emma Bell Miles merely insisted that they would eventually awaken to their full potential, which lay far beyond the boundaries prescribed by the stereotypes dominant then (and now). It was a reasonable, indeed even modest, goal. Toward such an awakening, Emma Bell Miles made a lasting contribution in *The Spirit of the Mountains*.

DAVID E. WHISNANT

Durham, North Carolina
March 1975

---

[24]Robert F. Munn, "Appalachian America: the Emergence of a Concept, 1895–1964," *Mountain Life and Work* 41 (Spring 1965), 7.

A BIBLIOGRAPHY OF EMMA BELL MILES

1904 "Difference" (poem), *Harper's Monthly* 108 (March), 653.

"Homesick" (poem), *Harper's Monthly* 108 (April), 789.

"Some Real American Music" (article), *Harper's Monthly* 109 (June), 118–23 (reprinted as Chapter VIII of *The Spirit of the Mountains*).

1905 "Red Wood Lily" (poem), *Century* 70 (May), 108.

"Hedge Bindweed" (poem), *Lippincott's* 75 (June), 768.

"Lost Comrade" (poem), *Harper's Monthly* 111 (July), 197.

"Mocassin Flower" (poem), *Century* 70 (August), 536.

The Spirit of the Mountains. New York: James Pott & Co.

1906 "Ironweed" (poem), *Reader* 7 (February), 286.

"After Reading Thoreau" (poem), *Century* 72 (October), 855.

1907 "Old House Dreams" (poem), *Century* 73 (March), 738.

"Banjo and the Loom" (poem), *Century* 74 (August), 650.

1908 "Common Lot" (short story), *Harper's Monthly* 118 (December), 145–54.

1909 "Broken Urn" (short story), *Putnam's* 5 (February), 574–80.

"A Dark Rose" (short story), *Harper's Monthly* 118 (February), 426–33.

"The Homecoming of Evelina" (short story), *Putnam's* 6 (May), 233–37.

"The Dulcimore" (short story), *Harper's Monthly* 119 (November), 949–56.

1910 "Flyaway Flittermouse" (short story), *Harper's Monthly* 121 (July), 229–35.

"Three Roads and a River" (short story), *Harper's Monthly* 121 (November), 882–89.

"Wood Smoke" (poem), *Harper's Bazaar* 44 (December), 736
(Caroline Wood Morrison, joint author).

1912 "Flower of Noon" (short story), *Craftsman* 21 (January), 386–94.

"At the Top of Sourwood" (short story), *Lippincott's* 89 (March),
393–402.

"Enchanter's Nightshade" (short story), *Craftsman* 22 (July),
387–97.

Chords from a Dulcimore (poems). Chattanooga: Drummer
Printing Co. [Eight poems: "Music and Fire," "The Candidate
at Caney's Cove," "Homesick," "The Stick Horse," "The Banjo
and the Loom," "Woodsmoke," "The Old House Dreams," and
"The Shadow".]

1914 Series of editorials and signed columns ("Fountain Square Conversations") in the Chattanooga *News*, May and June.

1919 *Our Southern Birds*. Chicago: National Book Co.; 2nd ed., Mor-
ristown, Tenn.: Globe Book Co., 1922.

1930 *Strains From a Dulcimore* (poems), ed. Abby Crawford Milton.
Atlanta: Bozart Press. [72 poems, including all of those published in *Chords from a Dulcimore*.]

D.E.W.

THE SPIRIT OF THE MOUNTAINS

KING'S CREEK

The Spirit of the Mountains

By
Emma B. Miles

NEW YORK
JAMES POTT & COMPANY
1905

First Impression, October, 1905.

THE AUTHOR wishes to thank MESSRS.
HARPER & BROTHERS for permission to
reprint the chapter entitled, SOME REAL
AMERICAN MUSIC, which appeared in
HARPER'S MAGAZINE, for June, 1904.

CHAPTER I

ON King's Creek there is a log house of one
large pen that is schoolhouse, church and
town hall, all in one, and thus easily the most
important building in the district. From its
door one looks across the slope of the Robbins
farm to the "breaks" of King's Creek gulch.
A similar slope on the opposite side displays the
farms of the two Maisey brothers lying side by
side, both together a mere kerchief-like patch
in the miles on rolling miles of woods. There
are log barns and houses on both of these, and
sometimes a smoke of cooking curls up in a blue
scroll among the pines, where otherwise one
would never suspect a house. These are the
only visible signs of human habitation. One

would say that no kind of public gathering could be got together in the log church.

But, listening for a day, even for an hour, to the sounds that echo in this cup of the hills, one comes to know that life is ever present. The evidences are faint and far, but the ear makes sure of them—yodeling and calling, barking of dogs, crowing of cocks in the early morning.

Listen!—a horn is wound away off toward the gap. An axe rings on the crystal of a winter day. Some boy must needs advertise his riches of both ammunition and corn whiskey at once by several shots fired in quick succession at nothing at all. Hoofs clatter over the shale at the ford, far below, and sometimes the music of a hunt or a dancing party continues nearly through the night.

Yet the most attentive hearkening would but poorly serve to prepare one's expectations for the crowd that gathers here once a month to attend preaching. And when a "big meeting," protracted indefinitely, is in progress, and the ox and mule teams stand hitched in the woods all about, while the smaller children sleep in the wagons, and neighbors enjoy a basket dinner together near the big cave spring, the number present is amazing.

The school, however, "fares but middling" in the matter of attendance. Confinement for an hour or two, with songs and the imminent expectation of somebody's "takin' a big through" of religious excitement to break the monotony, is not insupportable, but the necessity of keeping still in time of books and of applying all one's mind to lessons that may or may not be about what one really wants to know, is a grievous yoke, indeed. The path to the school door is one that few care to tread, with the boundless forest to choose from. So it is that, while I am fairly sure of meeting, morning after morning, a faithful ten or fifteen, most of the children hereabout run free as the fawns and cubs that they often capture for playmates—as timid, as lithe and about as intellectual.

Our log church stands in the forest. There is scarce enough space cleared around it for a playground. Woodpeckers drum on its roof in the daytime and whippoorwills sing there at night. Acorns drop upon it in October with resounding taps that startle all the little ones within. Its walls are laid of heavy pine timbers squared roughly and well notched together, the cracks chinked with chips driven in slantwise and daubed with native clay. There is no belfry. The door is at one end and the high pulpit at the other. At one side is a stone chimney, massive as a tower, whose fireplace on cold days seems about to swallow the huddled school. It requires the strength of all the larger boys together to bring in a backlog. When I was a child I remember a number of us, on the heels of some prank, once hid in its sooty depths from the wrath of the teacher, much as the Indians took shelter in Nickojack from the pursuing forces of Sevier. How could we have kept school without the aid of that hospitable cavern? We roasted nuts in it, and potatoes and apples, and pigs' tails, brought from home. We even boiled eggs there in a tin bucket when Mis' Robbins' old blue hen obligingly stole her nest under the floor. We watched the sparks fly up the chimney when we should have been studying; we told fortunes, making and naming marks in the ashes. And oh, the visions we saw in its smoke, the futures we painted in its ruddy coals!

Still it stands, the mighty chimney, and now it is I who must sometimes chase the little fellows, laughing and squealing, into its dark recess and out again. With so few pupils little discipline is necessary, and we often spend the hot afternoons of September outside, with our books—old McGuffey readers, blue-back spellers, Testaments or whatever comes to hand, scattered about on the ground. If the young minds wander afield with the scampering and flitting of little brothers of tree-top and burrow, what matter? Perhaps they learn at such times something not to be found between the covers of Webster.

As for that, our study is never confined to the text-book long. The first hour of our day is devoted to reading in four classes of different grades, the second to arithmetic in three. Then we spend about thirty minutes in drawing maps and talking about the country represented, a primitive method of studying geography, but the best possible in default of more expensive books. Next we write, either a spelling lesson or a composition on some outdoor subject, until it is time for the noon "ree-cess." Dinner, eaten in the shade outside, is over in a few minutes, and then playtime scatters the little folks through the woods, making playhouses and bending down saplings for "ridey-hosses," until it is time to recall them by rapping on the door with a stick, as if the hollow house were a giant drum. The afternoon is very much like the morning, except that there is a class in such grammar as we can manage without text-books. Last of all, I give them something to take home with them, to think over and dream about—an object-lesson, a story, a poem, or a simple talk on some bit of natural science.

This is our regular programme, but it has

many and frequent variations. Sometimes, instead of calling the primary arithmetic class, I set the little ones to playing "Hull-gull, handfull, how many?" That teaches them as much addition and subtraction as they would be likely to get by figuring on a slate. Or perhaps all the slates are brought out at once for such a drawing lesson as may assist the girls in designing their own blocks of patchwork. Or the whole school becomes drowsy, and can best be refreshed by learning a song. Old hymns, "O for a Faith That Will Not Shrink," "When I Survey the Wondrous Cross," are quite as new in this part of the world as "Recessional" or "The Palms," and far more acceptable to the home folks, who soon learn them from the children. There are some kindergarten songs, too, that are greatly enjoyed; "I Have a Little Shadow" is a favorite. But they wake to their brightest under the influence of "The Star-Spangled Banner," "Marching Thro' Georgia" or "The Red, White and Blue." For there is not one in the school but has spent many

[7]

a long winter evening in listening to the fathers' and grandfathers' tales of the war, and even the youngest here understands enough about taxes and pensions and voting well enough to feel that their great "gover'ment" is to be revered above all human things. And the older girls bring their knitting and sewing to school, so that I am able now and again to delight them with a new stitch or a fresh quilt pattern. Or the excitement of "cross-spelling" is asked for, an exercise in which all but the babes take part. Cliff Rogers has been our crack speller, but Jimmy Fetridge, the widow's boy, is making a better record every week. Some Friday afternoon he will turn Cliff down, and then we can soon challenge the school yon side the creek to spell against us.

When in November the low clouds roll across the mountain, darkening until not even the most experienced housewife can tell when it is time to set up dinner for her men-folks, we put the books away entirely and hear over and over again the tales we love best. Sometimes the

[8]

children, too, tell stories from the Bible or real local occurrences in the time of the Indians, or of the war, or curious adaptations of Cherokee tradition.

And on the Friday before the third Sunday in each month we sweep the floor and the yard, fill the fireplace with boughs of autumn leaves, branches of blossoming dogwood or azalea, fronds of cinnamon fern, or whatever is most beautiful in the woods at the time, and make the place tidy for Sunday's preaching. Then we "speak pieces" the rest of the afternoon. Our choice of these is limited to the contents of Webster's Speller and the McGuffey Readers, supplemented by the little copy of the "Child's Garden of Verses" it is my good fortune to own, so that we are sure of hearing the same good things pretty regularly every Friday. Some lad is certain to declare that in winter he gets up at night as earnestly as if he didn't eat two meals a day by lamplight almost the year round. Another chooses "Come, come, come, the summer now is here"—only he generally pronounces it

[9]

"summerny," and some one else starts out in a vigorous sing-song:

> "The lark is up to meet the sun,
> The bee is on the wing."

However, there are occasional surprises, mostly traceable to the mountaineer's Mother Goose. "I'm got a speak, too," urged little Osee Rogers once, and forthwith delivered himself:

> "Hey, little boy, where'd you git your breeches?
> Daddy cut 'em out and mammy sewed the stitches."

He was mortally offended by the shout that went up when he had finished.

The children are of all sizes, ranging from the wee ones too little even to say their a-b-abs, and only sent to school because, unless they are kept out of mother's way, sister will have to stay at home to help, to the big boys who were expected by their mates to run every teacher out of school—with open knives, if necessary. I do not know why I have never had any serious trouble with these last. It is strange that the unconquerable chief of this group should preserve, outwardly, the most correct behavior. He is seventeen, a true mountaineer, and has, I believe, a future before him, but I should be relieved at present to have him off my mind. He made it clear at the outset, in a fashion that perplexes me still, that he would have nothing more intimate than armed peace between him and the teacher. School had been going on for nearly a week, when old man Robbins knocked at the door to ask that I keep the children from running over his potato patch. Now, this was a reasonable request enough, and I spoke to the school about it at once. The mere mention of a wish on the teacher's part was sufficient for the majority. But this boy—merely, I believe, to see what would come of it, although his family may very possibly have some grudge against old man Robbins—leaped the fence next recess and walked deliberately into the potato field and out

[11]

again. A reprimand brought no response whatever from him, although he seemed not at all sullen.

"Cliff," I asked, "if you were the teacher, what would you do with such a boy?"

"I'd whup him," he answered, brightening.

"But you are too old to whip. Suppose, now, you apologize, and tell the school you won't do it again?"

He faced about and stood fumbling his hat a moment; then he concocted a little speech which I am sure furnished its maker with some satisfaction. He enjoyed what he was pleased to consider the joke on himself and on me.

"Can't you say you are sorry you did it?" I prompted.

"Why," replied he, "I reckon I could, but I d'know as I am!"

We both laughed. "Well, Cliff," said I, "if you've sufficiently aired your independence, you may go to your seat."

He has never repeated the offense, nor has he ever committed any overt act of rebellion. But

[12]

now and again he feels it necessary to give an unexpected dig of his independence into the ribs of his teacher, just by way of assuring himself that he could be a free man if he wanted to. I am certain that I have no better friend in the school.

All the children in the district are related by blood in one degree or another. Our roll-call includes Sally Mary and Cripple John's Mary and Tan's Mary, all bearing the same surname; and there is, besides, Aunt Rose Mary and Mary-Jo, living yon side the creek. There are the different branches of the Rogers family— Clay and Frank, Red Jim and Lyin' Jim and Singin' Jim and Black Jim Rogers—in this district, their kin intermarried until no man could write the pedigree or ascertain the exact relationship of their offspring to each other. This question, however, does not disturb the children in the least. They never address one another as cousin; they are content to know that Uncle Tan's smokehouse is the resource of all in time of famine; that Aunt Martha's kind and strong

[13]

hands are always to be depended on when one is really ill; that Uncle Filmore plays the fiddle at all dances, and Uncle Dave shoes all the mules owned by the tribe.

'Lectar Fetridge's children come in the morning from a cabin two miles away, with their scant dinner in a strong basket woven of white-oak splints. If the little feet grow tired, the ten-year-old mother-sister of the group cuts a stick-horse that prances gayly over the remaining distance with no thought of fatigue. She has all the pathetic humility and patience of a saintly grandmother, this child, and endures cold and hunger as a matter of course. Always she turns with her soft, shining smile and asks me to "come go home with her," the last thing before quitting the school doorstep. And poor 'Lectar is always so glad of company!

Coming back from the spring to-day I espied a little figure waiting beside the path, its arms folded, its face very stern, with chin up and eye-brows down—the personification of dignity at the mature age of seven.

"Waiting for me, Osee?" I inquired.

He was, but would not own it. "Thought I'd 'ist see if there's goin' to be any wild grapes," he said; and a few minutes after, stalking beside me: "Mother said tell ye to come home with us to-night and fix to stay a week or two."

So he waits again in the evening with the same ostentation of nonchalance, preserving his dignity until the last pair of bare feet have pattered down the path. Then he is fain to walk beside his teacher, prattling very much like any other child of the good things mother is going to have for supper and of the pigs in his father's pen.

"I'm got free little chickens," he tells me, "and one um's a pullet—or a hen, I do' know which."

But he stiffens perceptibly inside of his little homespun roundabout and breeches as we approach the log house in the orchard which is his home; and by the time his sister, that representative of the frankly emotional and inferior sex,

[15]

has run out to meet us with her pet rooster in her arms, he is all mountaineer again.

"Milly," he tells her, "I wisht you'd tell mother to hurry up supper. I'm 'ist goin' down to the barn with father and the boys."

Even his mother laughs as she comes to the door, her toil-worn, wistful face seaming into fine wrinkles of amusement at his baby airs.

"Does he ever want you to rock him to sleep?" I wonder, watching the sturdy little legs tramp off to the barn.

"Oh, when he's sick or tired he's right glad to be my little boy for a while," she answers. "But he's always a growed-up man ag'in he wakes up in the morning."

CHAPTER II

"Poor people has a poor way."

SOLITUDE is deep water, and small boats do not ride well in it. Only a superficial observer could fail to understand that the mountain people really love their wilderness—love it for its beauty, for its freedom. Their intimacy with it dates from a babyhood when the thrill of clean wet sand was good to little feet; when "frog-houses" were built, and little tracks were printed in rows all over the shore of the creek; when the beginnings of æsthetic feeling found expression in necklaces of scarlet haws and head-dresses pinned and braided together of oak leaves, cardinal flowers and fern; when bear-grass in spring, "sarvices" and berries in sum-

mer and muscadines in autumn were first sought
after and prized most for the "wild flavor," the
peculiar tang of the woods which they contain.

I once rode up the Side with a grandmother
from Sawyers' Springs, who cried out, as the
overhanging curve of the bluff, crowned with
pines, came into view: "Now, ain't that finer
than any picter you ever seed in your life?—and
they call us pore mountaineers! We git more
out o' life than anybody."

The charm and mystery of bygone days
broods over the mountain country—the charm
of pioneer hardihood, of primitive peace, of the
fatalism of ancient peoples, of the rites and
legends of the aborigines. To one who understands these high solitudes it is no marvel that
the inhabitants should be mystics, dreamers,
given to fancies often absurd, but often wildly
sweet.

Nothing less than the charm of their stern
motherland could hold them here. They know
well enough that elsewhere they might sit by
the flesh-pots. Occasionally a whole starved-out

[18]

THE OVERHANGING BLUFF, CROWNED WITH PINES

family will emigrate westward, and, having settled, will spend years in simply waiting for
a chance to sell out and move back again. All
alike cling to the ungracious acres they have so
patiently and hardly won, because of the wild
world that lies outside their puny fences, because
of the dream-vistas, blue and violet, that lead
their eyes afar among the hills . . .

The site of a cabin is usually chosen as near
as possible to a fine spring. No other advantages will ever make up for the lack of good
water. There is a strong prejudice against
pumps; if a well must be dug, it is usually left
open to the air, and the water is reached by
means of a hooked pole which requires some
skillful manipulation to prevent losing the
bucket. Cisterns are considered filthy; water
that has stood overnight is "dead water," hardly
fit to wash one's face in. The mountaineer takes
the same pride in his water supply as the rich
man in his wine cellar, and is in this respect a
connoisseur. None but the purest and coldest

[19]

of freestone will satisfy him; chalybeate, which the city people make so much of, is no favorite, except as an iron water spring or well is believed never to go dry.

Pure air is prized as highly as pure water, and a cabin door is always open, save at night or during the worst weather. This, with the cracks and "cat-holes" where the chinking falls out, naturally renders windows superfluous, and they are rarely found in the older houses.

Of course, many habits of cabin life would seem uncleanly to dwellers in a better civilization. But this existence is nearly as primitive as that of the Dark Ages, and primitive life is necessarily dirty, if for no other reason than that it is lived close to the ground. Nearness to the soil is not so much a mere figure of speech as we are apt to imagine. If you will think, you will see that this must be so.

When a man has not only the living to provide, but many of his farm implements and much of his furniture—tables, chairs, axe-helves, bread-bowls, cupboards, cradles, even looms and wagons to make with the help of a few neighbors—perhaps his own shoemaking and blacksmithing to do, and certainly fuel to haul and a crop to raise—where is his time for bathing? Where, indeed, is his opportunity, when all winter the only room with a fire in it is crowded night and day?

When the mother of his household has to pick and dry wild fruits; wash the wool, card, spin and weave it; make soap, hominy, butter, lard and molasses; take care of the meat when the men have killed and cut it up—yes, and raise poultry, *besides* all the ordinary care of a household; when, moreover, it is a very fortunate wife, indeed, who does not carry a considerable burden of duties properly supposed to belong to masculine shoulders, such as bringing wood and water, milking, and raising garden—with all this, oh, dear! how *can* she comb her hair every day?

And when, in addition to the endless toil, the land from which the living must be wrung is "so poor it wouldn't hardly raise a fight"—thus

[21]

enforcing the most petty economies of improper food and worn-out clothing—what wonder if there are not dishes enough to go around when company comes, and children must eat from their parents' plates or a wife drink from her husband's coffee-cup? I have seen a woman carry water, dress a fowl, mix bread, feed her cow and pick up chips all in the same big tin pan, simply because it was the only vessel she had; I have seen pies rolled out and potatoes mashed with a beer-bottle found in the road.

The wonder is that they do occasionally take a bath; that the cooking is frequently good; that milk-jars are sunned and scalded into irreproachable sweetness; that sedge-brooms are scrubbed to a stump every other week; that washing is done regularly at the spring, where, unless the woman has a washboard, a "battle-block" sits beside the tubs and the great pot mounted on a rude stone furnace. White sand is sometimes strewed on the kitchen floor and renewed from day to day; the iron cooking-pots and spiders are thoroughly burned to free them of rust and grease; and a barrel of lye soap is made yearly from wood ashes and scraps of pork waste. Lastly, the cleansing and ventilating powers of an open wood fire must be known to be appreciated.

Salt pork is the mountaineer's standby, and the dripping fried out of it is his butter, his syrup, his oil. Sometimes this grease is eaten clear, the biscuits being dipped into it, but it is more often made into a "white gravy" with milk and flour. But the poorest have not even milk.

When any member of the family is taken ill the first article of food thought of is an egg, but it is usually fried to the consistency of leather before it reaches the invalid. Babies from the first month are fed on anything they will swallow—grease, sugar or strong coffee. If you object, the mother points with pride to her sturdy older children, never reflecting that in such a severe weeding-out only the well nigh invulnerable survive. Nor are the mountaineers aware that they have, as a people, the worst

[23]

stomachs in the world, for dyspepsia in its various form is called, in nine cases out of ten, either consumption or heart disease—a mountaineer would be ashamed to succumb to anything less serious.

Civilization is not likely soon to remedy this evil, since it substitutes drugged whiskey for their own moonshine, and badly compounded plugs for home-grown "scrip" tobacco. It also introduces cheap baking powders and the salicylic acid which is so dangerously convenient in canning fruit.

Yet, though we violate every rule of hygiene, we are a strong people, sound of wind and limb, making light of hardship and heavy labor. A doctor is not thought of, except in cases of broken bones or actual danger of death; ordinary ailments and childbirth are endured as a matter of course. Starvation and exposure do sometimes bring on real consumption, but there are plenty of men seventy years old who can farm and plow and fell trees and haul wood, and rule the tribe they have raised, and get drunk as heartily as any young buck of the new generation.

There is a farm in Hallet's Fork where I love to visit. It has a charm for me quite apart from mere picturesqueness—it is not the artist who loves the country best. One of the finer phases of this wholesome life is the sweet hospitality of its people. My visit invariably extends for days beyond my first intention, and every hour is a delight.

I hear the day begin with the twitter of birds —wrens that are building in the porch eaves, martins in their high swinging gourds, and the bluebirds whose four sky-colored eggs are hid in a hollow apple tree behind the kitchen. The moon, peeled down to a thin shaving, has hung just over the sunset, and the night has been dark, but at last a dim light filters through the one small window, showing one by one the homely pieces of furniture and the hanks of "spun-truck" and carpet rags bunched like huge bananas on a peg in the wall. The house-mother, seeing the daylight, rises, and presently the shine of a pitch-pine blaze is dancing over the rafters until it shall be "put out by the sun." The stir of the household wakes the mother-hen that sleeps in the woodshed, and she leads forth her brood with clucking and cheeping; the house-cat and her kittens set up a cry; the dogs run in and out as soon as the latch is lifted; a flood of wakening sounds pour in from yard and tree-top; Bess and Piedy proclaim the smarting full-ness of their udders, and the team lifts a raucous bray as the boys open the barn door. The farm is awake.

Then, far away—as from another world—comes a different note. Faint as it is, it could not, were it a trumpet blast, more distinctly pierce the cloak of local interest. You are conscious of it at once, think you must have been deceived, listen eagerly—no, there it is again, unmistakable amid the conversation of coarser creatures—the hymn of the wood-thrush!

It thrills you awake instantly; you put the

night from your eyes and sleep from every muscle; you are at once ready for new and brave work, and your mind is freed from all impurities. The concerns of the farm, the daily round, seem trivial now; simple and wholesome indeed, but of little worth unless its meaning is rendered by the voice of yonder seer.

Scarcely caught by the most attentive ear, the cool, pure tones ring far down the morning from their source in the hidden woods. On the creek below the farm is a laurel jungle, its banks of bloom delicately rose-flushed; the moccasin orchid sits bowed in contemplation here, and the cucumber tree lifts its great honey-hearted blossom to the dawn. These, one may believe, hearken to the message of the singer; but the stable and kitchen and the scratching fowls will have none of it. So came the prophets of old to a people enamored of golden idols and fat priesthoods; so come great thoughts ever to the toiling world.

Now the sun rises, stands upon the hill-top, a red ball in the smoke of spring clearing. The table is set out on the porch and breakfast is ready: hot biscuit and butter and coffee, bulk pork fried in slices, soggy potatoes and the inevitable white gravy. At this time of year there is little left of the stored provender of last autumn, and the new spring vegetables have not all come in. The hard times have passed, but the table is still rather scantily laid.

When the housework is done and all the men of the place are away at their labor the old house settles to a sweet monotony that in after years lingers in the memory like a strain of music. Now the Baby would run away to aunty's were it not that she stands in wholesome awe of the old gander who patrols the creek path and hisses terribly. There is nothing going on. The hum of bees from the blossoming fruit, the shouts of plowboys across the fields and the ripple of the spring branch come pleasantly to the ear; and the sun shines through the one low, square-paned window in friendlier fashion than it uses in more pretentious abodes. Curtain or no curtain, is

[28]

the light through an old log-house window ever garish? How it warms the rich, sombre, smoky tones of the interior, and fills the rafters with greenish reflections from the hot light on the grass outside! There are three wooden four-poster beds in the main room, every one occupied at night, and every one covered with the intricately pieced and quilted comforts of which the humblest cabin boasts a few. There are also some wonderful homespun coverlets, beautiful with the dull dyes of barks, berries, copperas and indigo. There are three or four chairs bottomed with white-oak splints, one rocker, one rude table and some faded homespun rugs; there is a clock on the fireboard, flanked by a bottle of whiskey and a box of seeds; and that is positively all.

. . . Flies buzz; the tall clock ticks drowsily; a hound pads leisurely in to lie down under the bed; a frying chicken (the creature called a "broiler" in northern and eastern communities), camping on Baby's trail of crumbs, chirps querulously in the doorway. But the little girl

[29]

has fallen asleep in the grass, and is brought in and laid on the bed with a cloth over her face. The mother is crooning over her work, some old ballad of an eerie sadness and the indefinable charm of unlooked-for minor endings, something she learned as a child from a grandmother whose grandmother again brought it from Ireland or Scotland. As she bends above the loom, sending the shuttle back and forth, her voice goes on softly, interrupted by the thump of the batten:

"The cuckoo's a pretty bird, she sings as she
     flies;
She brings us good tidings and tells us no lies.

"Meeting is pleasure and parting is grief;
And an inconstant lover is worse than a thief.

"A thief can but rob you, and take what you
     have,
And an inconstant lover will bring you to your
     grave.

"Your grave will consume you and turn you to
    dust,
And where is the young man a maiden can
    trust?

"O, green grows the laurel, and so does the
    rue . . ."

The loom stands in the porch, shaded by hops
and honeysuckle, making with the woman's figure a cool silhouette against the sunshine.
Thump—thump—thump! What does she know
of lords and ladies, of cuckoo and nightingale?
These are mere words to the mountain people;
they will often stop to apologize, when asked to
sing to a stranger, for the lack of "sense" in the
lines; but they dare not alter a syllable; the song
is too anciently received.

By-and-by it is time to prepare dinner. The
kitchen is the oldest and the darkest portion of
the house, a sixteen-foot pen of heavy logs that
has stood for more than a hundred years. Its
walls are festooned with strings of peppers and
dried fruit; great gourds are hung about, one

[31]

containing lye soap, another salt, another crack-lings. Odd-looking utensils, these; boat-like bowls of maple for the kneading of bread, piggins and keelers of cedar, a wooden spurtle for stirring the evening kettle of mush, and a huge "gritter" on which green corn is grated in late summer for the making of "roas'n' ear" bread.

First the oven and its lid are brought out and heated on the fire to be filled with corn-pones— each oval pone with a hand-print conspicuous on its surface. Coals are spread underneath and piled upon the lid, and by the time the rest of the dinner is on the table the cornbread, too, is done. This method of baking is considered superior to any other, for meat and vegetables as well as for pastry and bread, since it allows neither steam nor flavor to escape during the process of cooking.

> "Sal's got a meat-skin laid away
> To grease her fryin'-pan every day."

Into the skillet are put thickly sliced potatoes to be half-fried, half-stewed; the earliest cucumbers and onions are sliced raw and salted; perhaps a pot of "wild salat" has been boiling for some time already, seasoned with a generous cube of fat pork, for "people that buy their meat by the quarter's worth can't eat pokeweed in their greens."

Last of all, while the men are washing their faces at the water-shelf outside the door, a mist-coated pitcher of buttermilk is brought up from the spring-house, and a bucket of blue cold water with a drift upon it of corn-silk and elder-flowers from the field.

Dinner is the midday event. When it is over the men return to their teaming in the fields and the women clear the table; then the house may drowse in the summer quiet all afternoon. A little breeze stirs between the open doors; cloud-shadows trail across the land; on the horizon fragments of rainbow span a deep-gray blur or passing storm. . . . The loom thumps patiently; there is an incessant murmur of water, wind, bees, or gentle rain—all the dreamy day . . .

[33]

At last the smoke of the supper fire hovers over the roof, a blue veil, and the evening work of feeding and putting away begins—"chores" is not in the local vocabulary. If the old man or one of the boys has been to the store Baby has now the delicious excitement of espying his return, running to open the barn gate and going through his few parcels of groceries. The chickens and guineas go to roost in the peach trees; the cows are milked at the gap and foaming pails carried back to the water-shelf; the sun is gone, and one lamp, with a broken chimney, is lighted and set on the supper-table. Far and clear in the dusk a whippoorwill is calling.

Night falls. Now the red glamour of firelight plays over the main room's rafters, and cotton is brought out and laid on the warm hearth for all unoccupied fingers to pick it, casting out the seeds. This is the social hour, when there is time for discussion and pleasant raillery and the barbaric jangle of a banjo or the less pleasing whine of a fiddle. At eight o'clock, however, it is time for bed.

[34]

So ends the day. Through the six narrow panes the night sky is visible, bent like a Madonna face over the slumbering earth. That ineffable tenderness, that enfolding peace—is it not the gift of nature to such simple ones as these?

Dear common things! Memories of hours of spiritual exaltation do not cling to the heart like the mere smells of hot meadows, of rain-wet plowed land, of barn lofts and kitchen corners. No mental awakening of adolescence weaves so close a raiment for the spirit in the after-years as the musk of mother's hair, the softness of her worn old apron and shawl. No literature can knit itself into our real being like the drowsy afternoons at home when nothing could ever have happened at all—the ceaseless blinking of poplar leaves, the croon of chickens in the hot dust under the honeysuckles. For to those who are the true home-lovers, home lies mostly in the kitchen and back yard.

Oh, the poignant sweetness, the infinite pathos of common things!

[35]

CHAPTER III

GRANDMOTHERS AND SONS

"There's more marries than keeps cold meat."

THE best society in the mountains—that is
to say, the most interesting—is that of
the young married men and that of the older
women. The young people are so shy that they
can hardly be said to form a part of society at
all. They are hedged with conventions and
meet almost as formally as young Japanese. For
example, on entering church the men are expected to turn to the left and seat themselves,
and the women to the right. It is permitted a
young fellow who is avowedly out courting to
sit beside his "gal," but I cannot imagine what
would happen if a young woman were to place
herself on the men's side of the house.

[36]

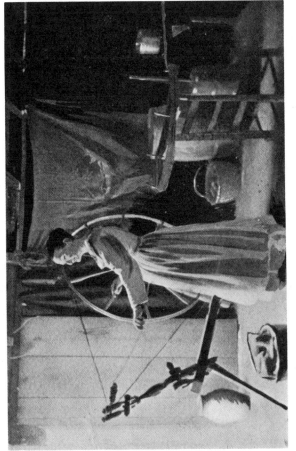

AUNT GENEVY ROGERS

After marriage something of the young man's shyness wears off; he gradually loses his awe of the opposite sex, and even within the conventions he finds room for intelligent conversation. Then he begins to be interesting, for his twenty-odd years of outdoor experience have really taught him much. As for the woman, it is not until she has seen her own boys grown to be men that she loses entirely the bashfulness of her girlhood, and the innate beauty and dignity of her nature shines forth in helpfulness and counsel.

I have learned to enjoy the company of these old prophetesses almost more than any other. The range of their experience is wonderful; they are, moreover, repositories of tribal lore—tradition and song, medical and religious learning. They are the nurses, the teachers of practical arts, the priestesses, and their wisdom commands the respect of all. An old woman has usually more authority over the bad boys of a household than all the strength of man. A similar reverence may have been accorded to the mothers of ancient Israel, as it is given by all peoples to those

[37]

of superior holiness—to priests, teachers, nuns; it is not the result of affection, still less of fear.

It was Lute Purvine—"Clodpoll"—who brought me word that Aunt Genevy Rogers was about to put a coverlet into her loom. As I had often expressed a wish to see a really fine web in the process of making, she invited me to come and watch the very beginning of the work.

"And she said to tell ye," added poor Clodpoll, "that Brother Absalom Darney's gwine to hold a feet-washin' at the Blue Spring Church a-Sunday and start a distracted meetin', and you can jist fix to stay with her while hit's continued on."

Protracted meeting in Rogers' Cove is indeed an inducement, but I could not promise to extend my visit so long.

Early next morning I shut the cabin door and took my way down the mountain. The path led for miles through the golden dapple of May woods. Rain had fallen in the night, and the trees stood immersed in a lake of thin mist, bluish, and shot with sunbeams. Cool wet leaves slapped softly together at my face and hands as I walked, and each step jarred down a shower of bright drops. Scarlet azaleas flashed in each thicket, and the pearly buds of the wild syringa were opening to show the pure pale gold of their hearts. The little sensitive-plant caught at my skirt now and again and dropped its leaves instantly, bearing erect only its pretty blossoms—balls of rosy fluff dusted over with gold. This plant is here known as shame-brier or stingy-vine; both names are highly suggestive of its sudden drooping or closing and drawing back. On Short Creek I found clusters of laurel and rhododendron buds, but neither had as yet come into bloom.

It was nearly noon when I turned into the Blue Spring road, and I hurried as well as I could in the warm sun, knowing that Aunt Genevy would be put out if I did not arrive in time for a warm dinner. I found her seated on the porch picking over a mess of "sissles," and she gave me her pleasant, quiet welcome without rising. Her daughter-in-law, Marilla, a woman of twenty-eight, who looks thirty-five, sent one of her own younger boys for a gourd of fresh spring water and placed a split-bottomed chair for me.

Aunt Genevy's house has two pens of logs, with a covered space between that is like a third room, but most of the time is spent by all the family out on the rude but ample porch along the front. A kitchen was to be added to the back of the house, and the men—Uncle Zach Rogers and Rilley's husband, his oldest son—were now "getting out" the logs for it, which means felling, scoring and rough-hewing the forty-odd eight-inch timbers required for its walls.

"So Rilley she's come up to spend the day," said Aunt Genevy, "and she'll redd up the dishes a'ter dinner while I git the chain ready."

Another visitor arrived in a few moments, a bare-footed woman, clad in a single faded calico garment. I learned that she was Mary Burns, and that her husband was helping with the logs. She sat on the edge of the porch, refusing a chair, as if accustomed to dropping down any-where. In spite of approaching maternity, to which she was evidently quite near, she was almost beautiful. I say almost, because she was hardly clean and her hair had not been combed in weeks—perhaps not thoroughly dressed since she was married.

"Air ye feelin' any better to-day, Mary?" inquired Aunt Genevy. "Law, I know jist how ye feel. Hit shore is miser'ble. The winter John was born we didn't have no turnips, nor 'taters, nor nothin'; the fence was so bad the hogs had broke in and eat 'em about all—and Zach he was away might' near all his time a-huntin' and cyard-playin' with a passel o' fool boys, and I had all o' my firewood to git, with jist what help sister Lou could give me—and Lou was jist a little gal then that I didn't dast hardly let go to the spring by herself."

The woman replied in a monotone slower and sweeter even than Aunt Genevy's: "I'm glad hit's hot enough so'st I ain't needin' any wood. I git chips over thar where Gid's a-workin' to

[41]

cook his meals; but hit shore gits away with me a-packin' water up the hill from the spring."

She looked up with a smile such as I have rarely seen on any but a baby's face, showing teeth as white and small as a child's.

"Yes, I know how that is, too," said the old woman. "When Lizzie was crawlin'—she was my second baby, the one that died—I'd take her and the bucket and start, and when I got to the top o' the hill I'd set her on the ground and go down to the spring, and git her as I come back. I always did think, though, hit was settin' in them damp bushes that started her to bein' sick all the time. Of course, I had to git water on rainy days the same as any others, and I was afeared to leave her in the house with the fire. I've knowed of two babies bein' burnt to death while their mothers was out a-workin' . . . Law, I know all about children, Mary, and work, too. Mine was never more'n two year apart. Don't you lose heart, Mary; there's better days a-comin' for ye whenever this is over."

She meant, as I discovered later, more than

she said in the last sentence. It was known in the neighborhood that Gideon Burns, although not a pronounced drunkard or villain, was cruel to his wife beyond what is usual to mountain men. He never struck her, or, if he did, it was not known; and Mary rarely complained. But the sympathy of the neighbor women was with her, and the more experienced hoped that the coming of the child would work a change.

Uncle Zach and the boys came in presently, and we all sat down to dinner round the table in the open entry. Rilley's three children ate with us, and some others I did not know, who had been playing about all morning. During the meal I noticed that Mary Burns was particularly urged to take her time and eat a portion of everything before her.

"Why, do you like them pickles?" said Aunt Genevy, as if surprised. "We're all tired of 'em; I put 'em on the table and they ain't tetched." This was not quite true. "I'll jist put the rest into a bowl for ye whenever ye git

[43]

ready to go home. Now, Rilley, don't ye let me forgit 'em. But don't you be in a hurry, Mary. I'm a-fixin' to put in some chain a'ter dinner, and you can stay and talk to me or Rilley, jist as you please."

The chain had been already spooled, wound on corncobs, whose pith had been burned out with the hot iron used by many instead of an auger, and the first thing now was to warp it. We placed the cob spools in the rack, carefully arranging their order, according to a diagram or "draft" which she assured me was over a hundred years old; so many of dull green, so many of blue, so many of copperas and creamy white. She drew a thread from each, tied the ends of all the threads, and fastened the knot to a peg in the upper corner of the warping-bars leaning against the opposite wall. Next, she deftly interwove the first cross in the threads, with fingers so nimble that I could not see how the trick was done. Then for some time I was of little service as she strung the chain back and forth, back and forth on the bars. Presently

[44]

Mary Burns joined us, gave us both, by way of greeting, her peculiarly sweet and childlike smile and seated herself in the doorway.

"Hit's gittin' hot," she complained; and presently said: "Mis' Rogers, I hate to be so much trouble to you'ns, but my head's achin' so bad. I'd like to git your comb a while to comb my hair. I had a tuckin'-comb a while back—hit ust to be mammy's—but them hounds o' Gid's chawed hit up last week."

Aunt Genevy told her where she might find the comb, and Mary brought it and let down her hair. What a web, what a cloak it spread over her shoulders! So matted was it that at first one could not be sure of its texture. But its color was chestnut, glinting gold, and its length and weight were extraordinary. I soon saw that she could never untangle it alone, and went to her assistance. Her pain must have been excruciating; in spite of care, handfuls came away by the roots. But she did not complain, and by patient persistence we straightened out the mouse-nests and witch-bridles lock by lock, until at last the

[45]

whole mass flowed smoothly, waving around her beautiful face.

Aunt Genevy was still walking slowly to and fro before her warp. The frame was two yards wide, and she stretched the gay strand three times across and added half a yard for "thrums," for eighteen feet was to be the length of her web. Then she would turn it back to the starting point again.

I have seen a bust of a Roman matron, mother to an emperor, which, with the addition of a few lines deeply graven by suffering meekly borne, would pass for a portrait of Geneva Rogers. But I have never seen anything greatly resembling Mary Burns. A certain maid once of the village of Nazareth may have had the same pure, modest sweetness, but her loveliness was of a type belonging to another race. For this Mary's hair, as I have said, was rich chestnut, and her eyes were blue—such a blue, softened by lashes of a length one notices on the lids of children. There was little light of intelligence in those eyes, but one felt that Mary's capacity for doglike devotion was unlimited. Excepting its innocence, the rich coloring of her face was its most striking feature. She had such a complexion as the first masters, knowing the effect of southern sun, painted without stint of olive and golden velvet and perfect rose. Gentleness and simplicity are characteristic of the faces of mountain girls.

There are those of a genuine exquisite modesty who have never in their lives slept in a room apart from the men of their household. But this was a child's face, with a child's ignorance behind its lovely mask, a child's readiness to flash into smiles at the least provocation, a face that ought surely to have met only with tenderness everywhere.

And with all her beauty she had not even the mountain woman's poor best of cheap calico to wear! I tried to imagine her dressed in a white dimity such as young girls wear in more favored regions, but even this seemed incongruous, although she could not have been more than seventeen years old. As we coiled and fastened her

[47]

hair I asked if she were going to the feet-washing, knowing how dear to the mountaineer heart is the privilege of attending every form of religious service.

"I reckon not," she answered, in her sweet, hushed, nun-like tones. "I ain't been to church sence my shoes wore out, some time last March." So she had trodden the freezing mud of early April with bare feet! It would never have occurred to her to hide her poverty or her present physical distress; she hardly realized that in this respect, also, she was ill-used by her husband.

At last the whole quantity of chain was drawn off the spools and doubled in one mass of six hundred threads nineteen and a half feet in length. This Aunt Genevy, having first carefully wrapped and tied the precious "cross" that preserves the pattern, looped up, loop within loop, until it lay at her feet in a great braid thicker than a man's arm.

Next we approached the loom itself and cleared it of the thrums that remained of her last web. Aunt Genevy then carried the big coil of chain to the back of the loom, loosened one end and spread it, securing the cross, on a wooden stake which she braced firmly against some sturdy little pegs let into the beam. Next the rake was hung immediately in front of the beam; this is a temporary affair which serves to keep the threads untangled, each "bout" of twelve threads being slipped separately between its wooden teeth.

Now we were ready to "beam" the warp. At first Aunt Genevy turned the heavy beam, and I, crouching behind the loom, held the strands taut as they uncoiled and spread themselves evenly on the slowly revolving beam, the rake combing them out like hair. We changed places as we tired. In spite of precaution, a tangle would arise at almost every turn of the beam, and often a thread would snap, and the broken ends have to be diligently sought out and tied, for an error of a thread or two here meant a flaw in the finished pattern. It was slow work, and required some patience, but at last the whole eighteen feet was wound on the beam, all but

[49]

the half yard or so that she left dangling over the rake.

"There, now!" I cried, triumphantly, "the great job's done."

"Oh, no," was the cheerful reply, "the great job's puttin' hit through them harness-eyes, and then after that they've got to go through the sley, one by one."

She lifted the rake now and laid it across the top of the loom, and then thrust a couple of thin laths, "bout-sticks," through the cross. It was now time to go about the night-work. There were the cows for Aunt Genevy to milk, and supper to cook for the men (all cooking, it would seem, is done "for the men"), and a hen was just hatching in the stable. Marilla and her brood were about departing, and Mary Burns had already taken her way along the short-cut that crossed the fields.

"Cain't ye stay the night?" was the inevitable invitation. And, when Rilley persisted in her refusal, "Well, cain't ye come back to-morrow, then? Anyhow, we'll all go together to the

[50]

feet-washin' a-Sunday. You come up afore supper; hit'll commence by early candle-lightin,' and
we'll want to take a soon start."

"How'd ye git on with your weavin',
mother?" inquired Uncle Zach, as he came in
to get the wash-pan. A young married man
never owns to the least interest in women's work,
but a patriarch like Zachariar Rogers, whose
dignity is too well assured to suffer through
trivial lapses, may display anything short of
affection toward his old woman, if he likes. He
may even assist in the cooking.

"Right well," was her answer. "That chain
beamed easier and went on better than any I've
put in the loom this year."

I had thought it was a fearful tangle, and I
am accustomed to handling yarn and carpet
spun-truck, too. I began to realize why the
mountain women are reluctant to part with
homespun coverlets at any price. But, indeed,
as Aunt Genevy had promised, worse was to
come.

Next morning a commotion in the road

brought me to the window. A man on a mule, riding without bridle or saddle, was scaring all the pigs and chickens round the barn gate. He had a tin bucket in his hands, and was thumping it to frighten the mule, that sidled and reared, only to be gripped into submission by the rider's strong legs. The fellow was ragged enough, but splendidly built and tall, with a strong, good-humored, rather sensual face.

That was all I had time to notice. He galloped on to the barn, somehow caused the beast to come to a stop with a plunge, and then sent a curious call or whoop ringing all over the farm. Seldom have I seen in a grown man such a display of sheer boyish spirits. Uncle Zach went to the barn and took charge of the mule, that, it appeared, had been caught straying near Burns' cabin, and the man strode away with his bucket. I heard him yodeling musically away through the woods.

"That's a sight of a feller, that Gid Burns," was the old man's comment as he came in to breakfast. "Said he 'lowed to git a bucket o'

water as he went back by the spring. Fust
thing I ever knowed him to do for that woman
o' hisn."

As soon as the breakfast dishes were washed
we went to the loom again, Aunt Genevy and I.
By the time we had untangled all the hanging
ends of thread preparatory to passing them one
by one through the heddles we were rather tired.
Putting them through occupied the rest of the
morning, particularly as a hundred and seventeen new harness-eyes, or heddles, had to be
made of scraps of carpet chain. This was work
I could do, and Aunt Genevy continued her task
of passing the threads through the loops, alter-
nating carefully, according to the nearly oblit-
erated "draft," between the different sets of heddles carrying the five separate layers of warp:
green in one, so many threads, so many vacan-
cies, blue in another, and so on.

When my heddles were finished I sat inside
the loom and handed her the threads. This is
the task most dreaded by mountain children.
Fancy being imprisoned in a loom all day hand-

ing those tedious threads! . . . And now I began to see the value of the "cross" in the chain, how it preserved the relative position of each and every colored thread in the complex pattern, holding every least stripe in place through all the yards and yards of seemingly hopelessly tangled warp.

"Warp's like people," said the dear soul, laughing quietly; "might' near all of us has to have a 'cross' to keep us straight."

She has had her share of crosses. For all her gentleness and courtesy, there is something terrible about old Geneva Rogers, a fascination, as of the stern and awful patience of some grand, stubborn slave. At an age when the mothers of any but a wolf-race become lace-capped and felt-shod pets of the household, relegated to the safety of cushioned nooks in favorite rooms, she is yet able to toil almost as severely as ever. She takes wearisome journeys afoot, and is ready to do battle upon occasion to defend her own. Her strength and endurance are beyond imagination to women of the sheltered life.

After dinner came a task only a little less tedious than that just completed—the drawing of each of those six hundred threads with a thin wooden hook through the fine rattan teeth of the sley. Here, again, the utmost caution was necessary to prevent any two threads from interlacing. Summoning all my patience, I began at one end of the sley and she at the other, and hours after we met rather on my side of the middle. As the sun was dropping behind the woods we stretched the threads forward four by four and tied them in place along the breast beam.

"Now at last you go to weaving," I said.

But she only smiled and showed me how even now all was not in working order. A few moments' trial brought to notice a loose thread or two, several twists, a "flat," and a broken thread to be coaxed into harmony with the rest. At last, in the fading light, Aunt Genevy proudly descended the stairs to finish the supper I had set on the fire, and announced that she would begin weaving Monday morning.

There was to be preaching Sunday morning

[55]

at the church, and we all made ready to go, Rilley and John and the old folks, the two younger boys and I. Mary Burns was sitting on her doorstep as we passed, and looked up with her smile.

"Has she no kinfolks at all?" I inquired. She had, it appeared, a father, and married brothers and sisters, living at some distance in the other valley; but she did not know how to write to send them a letter. They were honest people, said Uncle Zach. The oldest brother, a stonecutter, was well-to-do. Her father lived on his own farm. I knew better than to interfere by so much as a word, or I should have advised the poor child to make her way back to her father's house, where, by all the traditions of the land, she should have been well and tactfully received. But I do not think she would have wished to go.

Gid Burns was at church. He sat with the younger men of the congregation—that is, near the door, on the left. His elders and the pillars of the church, with a visiting preacher or two

[56]

and the man who was expected to lead the singing, occupied the front seats and the "amen corner." Aunt Genevy walked straight up to the front. Rilley and her children sat a little way behind her. The boys did not come in at all, preferring to remain with their fellows outside until the last bell rang, when they would slip quietly into the rearmost seats. Thus is precedence managed in the mountains.

Burns added a rich and powerful untrained tenor voice to "Some Have Mothers in the Promised Land," and seemed very attentive to the sermon. When meeting was out he was invited to a seat in our wagon, and accepted courteously and promptly. He and Uncle Zach exchanged views on the preacher's doctrine, and, although neither could read, they quoted a number of texts with tolerable accuracy, while we women and Rilley's children remained meekly and decorously silent.

The incompatibility of Gid Burns' religious pretensions with his habit of living struck nobody. Had their talk been of the coming elections, the subject would hardly have seemed less foreign to the question of daily behavior. In some respects the Scriptures influence the mountaineer's every-day behavior to a painful degree. On other matters of some importance its canons do not seem to bear at all. A man who would be shocked at swearing or Sabbath-breaking may make light of killing an enemy who has robbed or insulted one of his kin, his line of thought in the latter case being that when human creatures sink below a certain level they become mere vermin, of which the world needs immediate riddance.

I once heard a murderer awaiting trial say of the man he had killed: "I tell you, sir, as sure as God made apples, a meaner man never broke the world's bread. The only reason he hadn't died long ago was that God didn't want him and the devil wouldn't have him."

In the same abstract way Gid prated on of righteousness, temperance and judgment to come, without a thought of his own selfishness, since the victim of it was only a woman, and his

[58]

wife at that. The adolescent male of the human species has, even under civilization, an inborn contempt for girls. And this feeling in the mountaineer's maturity is superseded by a sort of wondering, half-amused pity. In Gideon's mind the pity had not yet arrived.

His strong teeth flashed, his eyes gleamed as he talked. There was undeniably a certain charm about him. He was simply a young savage with an overabundance of energy.

As we neared his hut a smoke of cooking rose from its chimney. Gid leaped over the revolving wheel, inviting us all in to dinner, as part of a habit of hospitality. I do not think he realized that acceptance was out of the question. Through the door I saw poor Mary, stooping painfully over her fire of gathered chips, sick, overheated, and probably suffering in ways of which we did not know. A few hours later she sent a little neighbor girl in haste to Aunt Genevy.

I would have accompanied Aunt Genevy to the hut across the fields, but was required to stay

[59]

and set up supper for Uncle Zach and the boys, who wished to go back to the feet-washing that night.

At last, when the night-work was done and the table cleared—the boys helping me far more than they were wont to help their mother—I was free to take my way through the soft dusk to Burns' cabin. I was ready to cry with anxiety. Aunt Genevy opened the door for me, and as she drank the hot coffee I had brought I heard the faint mewing of a new little voice. She and Mary had got through the awful hour quite alone—Gid had not put in an appearance since dinner—and she had just completed the dressing of the baby with such old flour-sacks as lay at hand. There was no light save a lantern that was used for 'possum-hunting in 'possum-time. The new mother moaned bitterly on her wretched pallet. A kettle of steaming water sat on the stones which served the purpose of fire-irons, and this I was bidden to replenish. Next I took charge of the little one, while Aunt Genevy, herself weary almost unto death, less-

[60]

ened the woman's discomfort as far as was possible.

At ten o'clock or thereabouts she told me I might go. "And send down Zach or Luther with some things you'll find tied up in a bundle under the head of my bed—jist as soon as they git home. I was aimin' to fetch 'em, but I forgot."

"Can't I bring them and stay with you?" I asked.

"You'd best git the boys and Zach some breakfast in the morning, if ye will," answered this old mountain woman, ever mindful of her man's comfort, although her own loss of food and sleep might be making her faint. And so I left, promising to bring her and Mary some breakfast before sunrise.

Gideon, having been informed by Uncle Zach at church of what was probably taking place at his house, did not return that night. But he was there before me in the morning. The breakfast I had carried across the field was not more than enough for two, but he accepted a portion when

[61]

it was offered him, Aunt Genevy declaring that she had slept several hours and was able to go home for her breakfast by-and-by.

"You hain't never looked at this big, fine boy yit," she said, with a little diffidence, and threw the door wide open for the sake of light as Burns, awkwardly and reluctantly, tiptoed to the bed. Mary raised the blanket, and the man peered down at the brown-velvet skull and red, wrinkled forehead which alone were visible.

"Hello, Buster!" he said, clearing his throat huskily. "Git up and go with pappy to ketch a 'possum!" Then he let down the ragged blanket gingerly and inquired: "Ain't he liable to smother? And then: "Hain't ye got nary dress that'll fit him?"

"I ain't got nothin' to make one out of," answered his wife, with the indifference of weakness and, I thought, despair.

Indeed, I felt my own sensibilities numbed by his lack of concern in the matter. He meandered about the room a little, evidently ill at ease, and

[62]

suddenly broke out: "Well, I expect I'll have to go to the store."

And then I could have boxed his ears.

But he went on, still with the same unconcern of manner and immobility of countenance: "I'll git this big man a suit o' clothes. Anything you want from thar, Mary?"

The woman's lids flew wide and a sudden radiance dispelled the weariness on her face. I wondered anew how the man could fail to be charmed by her beauty. I should have known that the first bond established between the primitive mother and her baby is that of being alike temporarily repulsive to their lord and master, and so companions in crime. She answered, quicker than I had ever heard her speak: "Yes, Gid; I want me a tuckin'-comb and some crackers and—and—a pair o' shoes."

She need not have faltered over the latter request. Gideon merely extracted a handful of small change from his clothes, counted his two dollars and odd cents deliberately, and said: "Well, I expect this'll git 'em, and some dinner besides. Much obleeged to you'ns. I'll git back ag'in dinner-time." And he shut the door behind him.

"Praise God!" muttered the old woman.

I looked at Mary Burns. Her face had taken the expression of a happy child's, and she was gazing at the little elevation of the blanket beside her. Then, because it was imperative I should go home that morning, I left them there together, the old woman and the young; the one with her hardships and suffering like a lesson learned and mastered, the other with her eyes just opened on its meaning.

I have never seen Gideon Burns nor his wife since that hour. But I have seen hundreds like them in the mountains, hundreds robbed of life's sweetest gift by the continual failure of well-meant efforts to bridge the gulf fixed by the mountaineers between woman and man.

At twenty the mountain woman is old in all that makes a woman old—toil, sorrow, child-bearing, loneliness and pitiful want. She knows

the weight not only of her own years; she has
dwelt since childhood in the shadow of centuries
gone. The house she lives in is nearly always
old—that is to say, a house with a history, a
house thronged with memories of other lives.
Her new carpet even, so gay on the rude pun-
cheons, was made of old clothes and scraps of
cloth. Who wove the cloth? It was woven on
her grandmother's loom. Yes, and she knows
who built the loom. The marks of his simple
tools are on its timbers still. Into her pretty
patchwork she puts her babies' outgrown frocks,
mingling their bright hues with the garments of
a dead mother or sister, setting the pattern together finally with the white in which she was
married, or the calico she wore to play-parties
when a girl. Perhaps she keeps her butter in a
cedar keeler or piggin that her grandfather
made. At all events she churns it in a home-
made churn. Her door swings on huge wooden
hinges. Who made them? In what fray was
the oak latch dented and split, and who mended
it with a scrap of iron? How many feet have

worn down the middle of the doorstep-stone! How many hearth-fires have sent their smoke in blue acrid puffs to darken the rafters! How many storms have beaten the hand-cleft shingles of the roof and strained at the mortised joints of its timbers!

Thus it comes that early in childhood she grows into dim consciousness of the vastness of human experience and the nobility of it. She learns to look upon the common human lot as a high calling. She gains the courage of the fatalist; the surety that nothing can happen which has not happened before; that, whatever she may be called upon to endure, she will yet know that others have undergone its like over and over again. Her lot is inevitably one of service and of suffering, and refines only as it is meekly and sweetly borne. For this reason she is never quite commonplace. To her mind nothing is trivial, all things being great with a meaning of divine purpose. And if as a corollary of this belief she is given to an absurd faith in petty signs and omens, who is to laugh at her?

Is it sickness? How many have lain in agony unto death on her old four-poster bed! Has her husband ill-treated her? She can endure without answering back. She has heard her elders tell of so many young husbands! Her dead babe? So many born here have slept and laughed for a time beside that hearth and dropped from the current of life!

She has heard the stories of everything in the house, from the brown and cracked old cups and bowls to the roof-beams themselves, until they have become her literature. From them she borrows a sublime silent courage and patience in the hour of trial. From their tragedies she learns, too, a sense of the immanent supernatural. It is almost as if they were haunted by audible and visible ghosts. Who would not fear to sit alone with old furniture that bears marks of blows, stains of blood and tears? They are friendly, too. They stand about her with the sympathy of like experience in times of distress and grief. This is one of the reasons why a mountain woman usually shows a disproportionate reluctance to selling her spinning-wheel or four-poster, even though the price offered be a bribe beyond imagination to one who sees whole dollars every day.

Few of these things become part of the man's life. Men do not live in the house. They commonly come in to eat and sleep, but their life is outdoors, foot-loose in the new forest or on the farm that renews itself crop by crop. His is the high daring and merciless recklessness of youth and the characteristic grim humor of the American, these though he live to be a hundred. Heartily, then, he conquers his chosen bit of wilderness, and heartily begets and rules his tribe, fighting and praying alike fearlessly and exultantly. Let the woman's part be to preserve tradition. His are the adventures of which future ballads will be sung. He is tempted to eagle flights across the valleys. For him is the excitement of fighting and journeying, trading, drinking and hunting, of wild rides and nights of danger. To the woman, in place of these, are long nights of anxious watching by the sick, or of waiting in dreary discomfort the uncertain result of an expedition in search of provender or game. The man bears his occasional days of pain with fortitude such as a brave lad might display, but he never learns the meaning of resignation. The woman belongs to the race, to the *old people*. He is a part of the *young nation*. His first songs are yodels. Then he learns dance tunes, and songs of hunting and fighting and drinking, and couplets of terse, quaint fun. It is over the loom and the knitting that old ballads are dreamily, endlessly crooned. . . .

Thus a rift is set between the sexes at babyhood that widens with the passing of the years, a rift that is never closed even by the daily interdependence of a poor man's partnership with his wife. Rare is a separation of a married couple in the mountains; the bond of perfect sympathy is rarer. The difference is one of mental training and standpoint rather than the more serious one of unlike character, or marriage would be impossible. But difference there

[69]

certainly is. Man and woman, although they
be twenty years married—although in twenty
years there has been not one hour in which one
has not been immediately necessary to the welfare of the other—still must needs regard each
other wonderingly, with a prejudice that takes
the form of a mild, half-amused contempt for
one another's opinions and desires. The pathos
of the situation is none the less terrible because
unconscious. They are so silent. They know
so pathetically little of each other's lives.

Of course, the woman's experience is the
deeper; the man's gain is in the breadth of outlook. His ambition leads him to make drain
after drain on the strength of his silent, wing-
less mate. Her position means sacrifice, sacrifice
and ever sacrifice, for her man first, and then for
her sons.

CHAPTER IV

NEIGHBORS

"Hit's worth a trick to learn one."

THERE is no such thing as a community of
mountaineers. They are knit together,
man to man, as friends, but not as a body of men.
A community, be it settlement or metropolis,
must revolve on some kind of axis, and must be
held together by a host of intermediate ties coming between the family and the State, and these
are not to be found in the mountains. A center
might be supplied by their common interest in
things not of earth, if the church met together
regularly, week after week, as in the towns; but
a body that beholds itself, as it were, but once
a month—and that always "if no providential
hinderance"—cannot exert much influence as a
bond.

[71]

Our men are almost incapable of concerted action unless they are needed by the Government. The traditions of the Revolution, persisting through generations, send them headlong into every war in which the United States becomes concerned. It was the living spirit of '76 that sent the mountaineers into the Civil War—they understood very little of what it was all about. I even venture to say that had the Southerners fought under the Stars and Stripes, most of our people would have been found on that side, following the flag they knew.

But between blood-relationship and the Federal Government no relations of master and servant, rich and poor, learned and ignorant, employer and employee, are interposed to bind society into a whole. In many localities currency is almost never used; a man gets his entire living from the ground, his utensils and implements are made by the local smith, and he barters pelts and beeswax for the needles and salt he must obtain at a store. Of course, this lack of commercial medium makes against the formation of castes. In short, the only classification is founded on character, and the only groups are those arising from ties of kinship.

We who live so far apart that we rarely see more of one another than the blue smoke of each other's chimneys are never at ease without the feel of the forest on every side—room to breathe, to expand, to develop, as well as to hunt and to wander at will. The nature of the mountaineer demands that he have solitude for the unhampered growth of his personality, wingroom for his eagle heart.

Under the conditions of such a life it is inevitable that our social grouping falls naturally into tribes and clans. Most of the man-handlings and murders in the mountains are the result of family feuds, of *perverted* family affection. For clans are ever pitching against one another, and up to a certain point intermarriage only makes things worse. If well-disposed and law-abiding, the factions seek to settle difficulties as amicably as possible. But some bully on the lower and more aggressive side is likely, after more or less corn whiskey, to open hostilities, fortified in the belief that he "can whip a field full o' them acorn-fed critters and mind three gaps at the same time." Very soon both parties are shooting at sight. How beautiful this very clannishness may be in its right sphere—how loyal and generous and kindly a tie—is known only to those who have depended on it through many a crisis of want and illness and sorrow, when half a county shared, in greater or less degree, the shock and the burden of tears and pain.

How different from the actual state of affairs is that widespread popular idea, fostered by newspaper stories, that no class of people in America is more lawless than the mountaineers! That more killings do not occur in the mountain country in proportion to the number of inhabitants than elsewhere is a fact beyond dispute. The process of law in these thinly settled places is likely to be tedious and uncertain, thus lending license to such as are by nature of a criminal tendency. This is the reverse phase of that unbounded personal liberty, that freedom for in-

[74]

dividual development, which a new country always affords, and which is bound to result in crime as well as in splendid, unique "types." But crime, as such, is not condoned by any mountaineer worthy the name. The criminal belongs to the submerged, the unwashed, the unfit, and is, besides, hopelessly in the minority. It is only the desperado here and there who figures so conspicuously in the newspapers; the peaceable many are unknown to the public. Then, too, it makes a difference who is killed. If you read that no attempt has been made to bring the murderer to justice, you may be reasonably certain that the dead man was not valuable to his neighborhood.

"There's places in Sand Mountain," in this region and that, where dirt and disorder, moral and material, reign rampant, and where the most extreme statements of the newspapers hold good. There is certainly a class of mountain people, dirty, degenerate, incredibly ignorant and unintelligent, very little superior to savages. It exists, but I have lived in many different lo-

[75]

calities in the Kentucky and Tennessee mountains and have never seen it yet. One of the members of the Blue Spring Church is said to have come, fifteen years ago, with his wife, both barefoot, penniless and horribly unclean, from such a haunt of squalor. That man does not amount to much yet, and in all likelihood never will, since he regularly drinks up his earnings; but he has at least acquired the accomplishment most valued by the mountain people, reading the Bible, and it is pleasant to visit his orderly cabin, gay with flowers, having a room set apart for the daughters of the family, and by them perpetually swept and garnished. I feel sure that there are many more of their kind who need only a chance to right themselves.

I once attempted to pay a long-promised visit to the family of an old farmer-preacher in Sequatchie, rider of a circuit on the river below Moccasin Bend. The road proved to be longer and harder than I had anticipated. So after the day's journey I found myself caught by the darkness in a strange part of the country, with no feed for my horse, and a stormy night approaching. I applied for shelter at the first dwelling, and was, of course, without comment, made welcome. Thus much I had expected, but was surprised when my host called me by name.

"Don't you know me?" he asked. "Don't you rickollect Tommy Bannon? Well, I'm his uncle Zebedee. Ain't you never heard Tommy call my name?" He was even more solicitous for my welfare than is usual here, and presently recalling that months ago I had assisted one Tommy Bannon out of an ordinary lad's troubles, I understood his uncle Zebedee's attitude. My slight service to the nephew had, according to an admirably simple view of human relations, placed me in line with the good people who made up the vast majority of the uncle's world, people to be trusted and cultivated as friends. It was inconceivable that I might belong to the dark minority of evil!

This man's big, double log house stood in the middle of a fine farm. It was a structure of the right sort—two pens, with an entry between,

[77]

every log "saddle-notched" to the next, making a sort of dovetail in the corners, and every timber set in a mortise and tenon. It was the kind of house that a tornado might roll over and over in one piece and leave about as solid as before. The barn and cellar were well stored. But the home was at such a distance from any market that the modern conveniences were few—a typical condition of affairs. Clothes and bedding, for instance, were mainly homespun and of excellent quality, but there were not enough dishes to enable all the family to eat at once. The sugar had given place to sorghum and honey, while there was imminent danger of a salt famine.

"Them folks down the road got no salt, either? I 'lowed ye might borrow a teacupful," I heard the man say to his wife.

"I've done sent thar," she answered, scraping the bottom of the salt-piggin. "And I know sister Jane ain't got none, for she jist yistidy tried to borrow some o' me!"

And it rained and rained. "I declare, pap,

[78]

you-uns had oughter ketch out the mules and git a soon start for Dunlap in the morning," said the wife, anxiously; but a record-breaking rain fell in the night and the river came up over its bridges. I could not get out, either to go on my way or to return, for another day and night. Nor was any salt to be had for our potatoes.

At my departure I begged to be allowed to pay at least for my horse's feed; but the answer was, "Why, no; I knowed you as soon as you come in!" as if that settled the matter beyond further parley. I doubt if an entire stranger would have been actually permitted to make payment; but my host assumed the obligation as a family affair.

The New Englander's suspicion of a gift has no place in the mountaineer's mind. He is not afraid of an obligation, and never dreams of looking for a worm of ulterior motive at the core of a kindness. Even candidates for local office have hardly learned the use of free drinks in electioneering.

Send your neighbor in the mountains a pres-

[79]

ent, and he will, if possible, return you something in the same basket. He has no notion of paying for the gift, neither is he striving to impress you with his independence, which is too fundamental a quality to need showing forth in such a paltry manner. The value of the gift has nothing to do with it. Perhaps what you gave him was costly—some store-bought article, and therefore doubly precious in his eyes. His return may be a fat shoat or a newly killed 'possum, or only a pumpkin or a cup of muscadines. However poor it may be, he is not ashamed of it. He has not looked at your gift so much as at the spirit of its offering, and he expects the same high-minded acceptance from you. A pumpkin, he argues, serves to express good feeling as plainly as a fatling heifer, provided it be his best.

The little boy who stood by my school-teacher's desk every morning last winter, complaining "I'm so hungry," until it became the rule for him to share the contents of my basket—how royally he presented me with the sweetbreads

[80]

when his father's only sow was made into winter provender! There, at last, was something he could share with his teacher. Kindliness for kindliness: that was his one thought, and neither he nor his parents would ever have dreamed of the giving of bread in any other than a spirit of fellowship and goodwill.

So borrowing and lending, bestowing and receiving, go merrily on, with very little of the friction that would certainly ensue in a more populous region. These good folks are narrow without being petty. Moreover, they see each other so infrequently, and are habitually of so few words, that the fine reserve of their manner is never displaced by too common familiarity.

Occasionally a mild covetousness will find frank expression, as, for instance: "John, I wouldn't care if I had that cow o' yourn and you-uns had ye a better one." But property rights are well respected, with some curious reservations. No woman will borrow another's wire hairpin without asking leave; no man will help himself to a friend's matches for his pipe;

[81]

these things have to be paid for at the store. But apples are plenty and neighbors few, and there is little objection to your climbing anybody's rail-fence and eating your fill. It is significant that, while those who need food frequently help themselves to it, robbery and housebreaking are almost unknown. On hot nights the cabin door stands wide open, and the only locks are those remarkable contrivances of hardwood, mysterious as the combination of a safe, that each fashions to his own liking for the smokehouse door.

And feuds are part of the price we pay for the simplicity and beauty of mountain life—for its hospitality, for its true and far-reaching family ties. I do not say the inevitable price, for the lawless fighter, along with illicit whiskey, is bound to disappear; but these ugly features are, under present conditions, the price of the tribal bond.

CHAPTER V

THE SAVAGE STRAIN

"The less a man talks, the fewer lies he tells."
—*Sayings of Joe Winchester.*

WHEN Joseph Brown's party wore their coonskin caps down to Nickojack, they, and the first pioneers that followed them, were not widely different from the settlers of older States. They brought with them plenty of New England shrewdness and grit, and these qualities persist in their descendants to-day. But vast modifications have been wrought, until the present type is scarcely to be traced to its original. The mountaineer is, generally speaking, even narrower and more superstitious, because more ignorant, than the farmer of the Adirondacks. He is also more generous, and this may

[83]

be due to the frequency with which cold and hunger beset him. For if a man is not sure when his own time may come to beg, he is careful how he refuses his neighbor. And, except along the coast, where men are wont to meet the sea in its rages, there is hardly a New Englander as daring, as reckless of danger to life and limb, as are the mountaineers; but it is easy to see that this trait, too, is directly the result of environment.

But there are other qualities and traditions the cause of which is farther to seek. The bearing of the mountaineer, for instance, dignified rather than stolid, distinct alike from the homely shrewdness of the New Englander, the picturesque freedom of the man from the new West and the elaborate courtesy of the South proper! Does it not bring to mind a vision of moccasined feet and the grave, laconic speech of chiefs met together for a high pow-wow?

A little boy ran out on the porch to meet his father just returned from town. He cried out in the delicious excitement of a child ready to

[84]

burst with news: "Father! Jim's married, and old June's got a calf, and we bought a barrel o' specked apples!" The man gave him just a glance and an inarticulate murmur in passing. He was not ill-natured; had the little fellow been a few years younger he might have received the compliment of being laughed at, and a whimsical reply, "Ah, now, that ain't all so, is hit?" But he was considered old enough to know better, and it became necessary to snub him.

Under such treatment a lad soon attains the sedate demeanor of his elders, and at fourteen chews his tobacco in a wordless revery with as much dignity as a young brave in his first war-paint.

Indian-like, too, is the mountaineer's stoic acceptance of privation and hardship and the sardonic quality of his humor. From the Cherokee came most of the mountaineer's knowledge of herbs and medicines. The best herb-doctor I know is a dear old soul who learned from an Indian doctor when she was a child, rambling with him and his children in search of simples.

[85]

And, of course, their woodcraft is Indian—the thousand contrivances of the naked man cast on his own resources in the forest. The savage had reduced the art of living and traveling in the wilderness to an exact science hundreds of years before his white brother had need of it. And with all his knowledge the white man could not better so finished a product, could only borrow it outright and in detail.

I once accompanied old Pap Farris on a tramp around his land. He had recently had the whole tract "processioned," to make sure of some disputed boundaries, and was going over them to fix them in mind. He pointed out to me the cornerstones, and now and again a "line tree" marked after the Indian fashion with an almost indistinguishable scar in the outer bark. A white blaze, such as is used for the marking out of new trails, reaches through to the growing sap, and is usually covered over by the time the trail is trodden clear enough to do without its help. But a line-mark must be referred to year after year. We had just traversed a thicket of "little

[86]

timber," grown up, since the war, on land that had once been cleared, when he paused in the edge of the older woods and called my attention to an ordinary-looking stone. It was not a landmark, but he stooped over and raised it. There was a hole underneath which might have been made by a snake or a mole, for what I could see. But Pap said, "Now I'll show you-uns somep'n," and thrust his walking-stick of seasoned hickory down and down. I do not know what I expected to come wriggling out of that hole. I was certainly surprised when he withdrew the stick dripping wet for about three inches from the tip.

"See that? All last summer, when there was springs goin' dry that hadn't failed in ten year, this stick fetched water here every time. If I ever do take a notion to dig hit out, hit'll be a fine spring."

The one subject the mountaineer allows himself to become enthusiastic over is cold water. I had often heard of the discovery and subsequent careful concealment of springs by old men,

[87]

but this was the first such secret I had ever been permitted to share. I asked why he hid his find. He would give no satisfactory answer, merely repeating, "Hit's a fine vein o' water, a fine spring."

To my thinking, the incident savored of aboriginal custom, and called to my mind a tale of hidden things which I heard first as a child, sitting on a sheepskin before the fire. I have listened to it often since, the story of the Winchester mystery, with but few variations. The mountaineer fixes a statement in his memory by reiteration, and seems sometimes not satisfied that you have fairly grasped his story until he has repeated it, in substance, several times. Told in this manner, a word or a song may pass from mouth to mouth and undergo but slight changing.

Old Joe Winchester was too much of a wanderer to have amassed any wealth of houses and lands. But he had the gathered experience of the rolling stone, and is remembered as an intelligent man and an interesting talker by many of the gray heads of our county. He was also an excellent worker in wood and iron, and to his ability in these lines may have been due, in the first instance, the fact that Salola chose him for his friend. Salola ("Squirrel") had returned from the nation to visit the country of his ancestors, and seemed deeply interested, in his immobile Indian fashion, in all Winchester's processes of molding and blacksmithing and tool-making. The two soon got into the way of disappearing together for weeks at a time, ostensibly on hunting expeditions. But when they had hunted and fished and trapped and drank and worked together by turns for several years a whisper went abroad that their long camping trips down the Suck and in the Horseshoe were not without purpose, that they were in search of something. Of course, a vein of ore was the first guess, although at that time nothing more valuable than second-rate coal was believed to exist in the mountain. Perhaps some, curious or covetous,

[89]

might have spied upon the secret, had not Winchester been well known for a quick-tempered man, whose rifle was ever ready; and the Indian's disposition was no less uncertain.

The two men were alike in many ways—both dark, spare, tall and silent-footed; both wearing moccasins, and armed with the long knife and tomahawk, carried in a stout leather belt. And both wore the hunting-shirt of scarlet homespun, comfortable as the modern sweater; scarlet, because "red makes the deer stand at gaze."

It was not until long after Salola had returned to his people that Winchester, gray now and with but little prospect of years in which to measure the value of his secret, opened his mouth in answer to the inquiries of his grown sons. Yes, he said, he was looking for a mine; and yes, he had found mineral. But if they were wishful for the like, they could e'en go hunt for it as he had hunted.

That was all he would say. So they were obliged to see the red shirt, Sunday after Sunday, disappear into the woods alone, now in this direction and now in that, but always returning with sufficient lead to make bullets for all their guns during the week. He mended nets and pans with that lead for all his neighbors, for he was an open-handed soul. But to none did he proffer a hint of the source's whereabouts.

One day a man threw the whole neighborhood into considerable excitement by proclaiming that he had found old Joe Winchester's mine. He had become separated from a surveying party, and while confused in mind and completely turned around as to the points of the compass, had come upon virgin lead lying right on the surface. He had broken bushes all about the spot, and had even blazed a number of trees to mark his trail. But, though he essayed again and again to retrace his steps, once attempting to pilot a company of seekers, he never found the place again.

At another time a hunter followed his dogs over a hill in the Suck region, down across a "swag," and over the breaks of the stream, before finally overtaking his quarry. Somewhere along this course he noticed where the deer's hoof had scraped a bit of gray metal that might or might not have been Joe Winchester's lead. He had not stayed to examine it, could not even remember on which hill it was; he was after that deer.

At first in jest, but later with some show of serious belief, it began to be said that the old man had received an enchantment from the Cherokee—some Indian "medicine" that would guard his secret forever. Winchester laughed at such talk when it reached his ears. "If you-uns want a mine, you're jist as welcome to hunt for hit as I was," he replied to all questions.

At last, when he was no longer able either to fetch his lead or to use it, he told his sons a tale stranger than any their imaginations had invented. He recounted to them the whole story of the six years he had spent with Salola; all their adventures in the forest, the bear and deer they had killed, the camps they had built of logs and bark and pine boughs, and the caves they had explored merely by the way. The boys'

[92]

curiosity about the old man's inexhaustible lead supply had no doubt prevented their ever guessing that the real object of his search was not lead at all, but a far more valuable vein of silver which had been known and worked by the Indians before they left Tennessee. Salola had by heart the traditions of the place as he had received them in boyhood from his elders, and these were all the two had to go on, no maps nor written instructions of any kind.

They had found, as Salola had predicted, the primitive tools that had been employed in working the ore, rusted and decayed. It is a pity the old man did not describe these more minutely. They were hidden in a rock-house that Salola believed to be about two miles from the real mine. For the abandonment had been premeditated, and arranged with a view to returning one day and taking possession; hence all traces of their not very extensive operations had been concealed. There was an Indian ladder—a pole with limbs lopped off so as to afford a foothold—leaning against the rock just about where the

Indian had expected to find it. It was almost too rotten to bear its own weight, and they had cut another, for the cliff was to be ascended at this point. Then, at the top, a stooping oak, bent over when a sapling, directed them a little farther.

After this they had lost the trail for three years, and had only found it by accident, stumbling one day into a cavern lined with picture-writing that not even the Indian could decipher. There was a rude outline of a chief with feathers and drawn bow. There were a number of suns, or moons, a bird flying, and some symbolic criss-crosses, which, according to Salola, signified camps, but nothing else that a man could make head or tail of. There were arrow-heads and potsherds on the cave's floor in plenty, and there was a circular pit, fire-blackened, that seemed to have been used as a forge or smelting-furnace. This was the most important discovery they made in all the six years.

And then, although they seemed just on the point of finding the object of their search, the

[94]

Indian gave over seeking. He was old; he felt death on him, he said, and wished to be with his people. Whether he had other reasons for returning to the nation, or whether he lost hope and faith in their quest, Winchester never knew. Nor did his own solitary ramblings meet with further success; the old silver mine was never found.

All that was mighty interesting, the Winchester boys admitted. But he had really told them nothing that would help their pursuit of the search. He had told all this simply as a tale, naming no localities, not even the general direction of such finds as he had made. Where had he come upon the cavern with the forge-pit? That was what they most wished to know.

"Well," he answered their eagerness grudgingly, "I will tell ye this much. You go down Tanner's Creek in the dry time o' the fall, when all the creeks run low, until you come to a curi's-lookin' blue rock in the bed of the creek that you can't see when the water's up; and thar ye leave hit and go up to the breaks, whar ye ought

[95]

to find our Indian ladder still a-leanin' into a corner o' the bluff."

"I don't much believe in that air mine," said one.

"I've seed the float," he answered, quietly. "Ol' Salola had a piece. Them Indians had kep' some all that time to prove the story; and hit sure was rich."

"You don't know whether hit come from that mine or not," they objected; but nevertheless they believed him.

"When he comes to die he'll tell," they said to themselves. But old Joe Winchester's end came as he would have desired, suddenly and without warning; and even the whereabouts of his lead is still unknown.

But the greater mystery to me is the old man's motive in burying his secret with him. Did the Indian forbid him by oath to divulge it? Did he wish to test the courage and endurance of his sons by obliging them to search? Did he, to the end of his days, cherish a hope of selling his information to some capitalist willing to invest?

[96]

Or did he always intend to tell them at last—some day—and put the day off too long? I have thought over these and other explanations, but they seem to me equally improbable.

It seems to me now, however, that if I could learn why Pap Farris conceals his vein of free-stone water I should have surprised the chief wonder of the Winchester secret. The recesses of these men's natures are not less wild and dark and tortuous than the labyrinths of their native hills. Sometimes one may suspect an aroma of Cherokee magic haunting them all.

CHAPTER VI

SUPERNATURAL

"I've swapped the devil for a witch."

EVERY phase of the mountaineer's life connects in some way with tradition anciently received. It is scarcely too much to say
that every man and woman in the mountains is,
in one way or another, superstitious. The "boo-
ger" may be dreams, or charms against diseases;
it may be some absurd fear, of owls, or haunts,
or burning certain kinds of wood, or carrying a
hoe through the house. It is sure to be something. You stumble on it some day, grotesque
as a Dutch toy, among the clean hard furniture
of a simple mind, and wonder how it came there.
From the old Irish it is likely, or else from the
Cherokee, or from the grimly mystical minds of
the earliest Indian-fighting pioneers.

[98]

AUNT NEPPIE ANN

The signs and portents at the end of every tongue are innumerable. If a bird or a chicken dies in your hand you will get the weak trembles and drop everything you take hold of. If a bird weaves a hair of your head into its nest you will have headaches until that nest falls to pieces; and if ever a bird builds in your shoe or pocket, or in any of your clothes, you may prepare to die within the year. If a man comes into your house first on New Year's morning you will have no luck that year in raising chickens; if a woman, your luck in boiling soap will be bad.

And so forth, and so on. "If you don't cuss you'll never raise gourds." "If you ain't bad-tempered you can't git pepper to bear." "If you're hairy about the arms and chest you'll have good luck with hogs." "If you cut up a feather-bed into pillows you'll have bad luck till they all wear out."

"If the bread's burnt the cook's mad." "If your fire won't kindle you'll marry a lazy man; if you slop water on your clothes you'll marry a drunkard." "If you dream o' flyin' "—— But let us not begin on the lore of dreams.

Curious, indeed, are the superstitions of grandmotherhood—the ceremonies and beliefs called into play by the arrival of new little grandchildren. What a plucking of herbs, what a consulting of signs and omens, both before and after the event! What pet names then and lullabies—baby-talk mingled with endearments that Chaucer's nurse may have addressed to him! "You little dawtie, little poppee-doll! Bless hits little angel-lookin' time!"

If the number of creases on each of the baby's fat legs is the same the next born will be a girl. The baby must wear a string of corn-beads round its neck to facilitate teething, and later a bullet or coin to prevent nose-bleed. Its wee track must be printed in the first snow that falls, to ward off croup. The first woodtick that fastens itself to the little body is an omen, too: you must kill it on an axe or other tool if you wish baby to grow into a clever workman. If it be killed on a bell or banjo, on any clear-ringing

[100]

substance, he will develop a voice for singing; if on a book, he will learn to "speak all kind o' proper words," all gifts highly esteemed in the mountains. A baby's sore mouth may be cured by the breath of a man who has never seen his own father. This I take to be an old Cherokee charm. Sometimes the child is given a drink from an old shoe. Few employ these remedies, however, so long as the bitter golden-seal root is to be had for the digging.

Old and young fear above all things the breaking of the Sabbath. Some fellows who are perfectly unconscious of any blame attaching to their custom of never working through the week, entertain such strict scruples on this point that their hard-working women folk are obliged to sit up late Saturday night patching clothes by the light of a pine knot, rather than touch needle and scissors, implements of labor, on Sunday. I once knew two toilers in an isolated bark camp to lose count, peel bark from morning till night on what they supposed was Saturday, and on discovering their mistake grieve as though for mortal sin. Were a man perversely to plow and plant a field on Sunday his neighbors would confidently expect a blight to consume that particular crop before it could be harvested. "No good was ever knowed to come of workin' on a Sunday."

When I visit Aunt Neppie Ann Lowry I try to make a point of staying over-night for the sake of her fine old stories. We sit by the light of a small lamp, instead of a pine torch, but the effect is not seriously marred.

Aunt Neppie Ann's lot is not so hard as that of most mountain women. Although she has been a widow these twenty years and has lost three children, she invariably states at experience meeting that her soul is happy and that she has a heap to be thankful for, which is quite true. She lives with her two sons; Joe's wife is dead and Arth is one of the few confirmed bachelors in this locality, and between them they make her a good living. She keeps the house, raises chickens and looks after the milk and butter.

Joe's fourteen-year-old boy gets in the night wood and the water, and even milks the cows. She does but little spinning and weaving, and no garden or field work at all. So she has more time for what stands to her people instead of literary pursuits—the repeating over and over of old tales and proverbs and the observance of signs and omens. On Sundays she goes attired in dark-colored homespun, with clean, starched apron and kerchief. Her sunbonnet is made of store gingham and stitched after an ivy-leaf pattern of her own. She has had it "for Sunday" for seven years come next November. She always carries a fan, the tail of a great wild gobbler that Arth killed one memorable Christmas week when some half-dozen hunters camped in Purvine's Fork and one froze to death. This circumstance gives the great turkey-fan a peculiar and eerie value in Aunt Neppie Ann's eyes. She carries, too, a reticule containing her spectacles, and sundry treasures of seeds and medicines, which she is in the habit of dividing with her neighbors on Sunday visits. She is ac-

[103]

quainted with some half thousand herbs and remedies, including what to wear round one's neck against contagious diseases and toothaches. Wherever trouble is present there enters Aunt Neppie Ann, stepping in comfortable state, her reticule packed with herbs and salves. To a death or a birth or an illness she comes in all the beauty of an angel of healing, and everywhere she is well beloved.

"I was a-comin' home from Partheny's yistidy," says she, "and I found this here pore little cat a-settin' on a log in the woods and a yowlin' like hit was might' near't starved. Hit's good luck to have a cat come to ye that a way, and this here one's a cat o' three colors. They say your house'll never burn down whilst ye keep one. I've took 'n' buried the tip eend o' her tail under the doorstep, so'st she'd stay." The old woman laughs placidly, for even to her this particular superstition seems a little absurd; still, there *may* be something in it, she thinks, stroking her pet thoughtfully. "I've seed people that believed black cats was witches, hain't you?"

[104]

"Witches! Shucks, mother!" snorts Joe at this, and then subsides. Joe Lowry will not send his boy to the Sunday-school the summer people have established at the Foot because too many unreasonable doctrines are taught there. He is aware that all the summer people believe the world to be round like a ball. Now, Joe is too hard-headed to believe even in witchcraft, much less in any such doggoned foolishness as that. He is sure his father and grandfather never heard tell of such an idea, and he can read with his own eyes what the Good Book says of the earth's four corners. The Lord certainly cannot have made the world over since that was written!

He believes, however—for he has noticed it all his life—that one must depend a great deal on the moon. In the first place, the new moon is full of water, as everybody knows; and if it stands on its tip so that the water spills out there will be a wet month. If it lies on its back it "holds the water," and there will be little rain. Cows are supposed to come fresh, and rainy weather to begin and end, on the change of the moon. Potatoes planted in the light of the moon run to vine and make no tubers. Pork killed in the light of the moon runs to grease, shrinking in the pan. Soap must be made just in the right time of the moon. Roofs must also be put on with reference to this, or the nails will draw right out of the wood and let the shingles fall. Even a "fence-worm" if laid in the wrong time of the moon is a failure; with frost and thawing the rails will surely sink into the ground.

Arth Lowry has worked in town off and on for some years, and is, in Joe's opinion, plumb spoiled for a mountain man. "I'll swar to Joshua, Joe," he says, "you're as superstitious as some ol' woman that smokes a pipe and don't know the war's over! If the moon knowed what all you-uns hold hit responsible fur hit'd git scared and fall down out o' the sky."

"Them town people all claims the moon makes the water o' the sea to rise an' fall. I don't see why they say hit can't cause Ir'sh potaters to run to vine," says Joe, in an injured tone.

[106]

"You may see for your own self when ye go through the woods that some logs lays on top o' the ground and others sinks in till they're might' near buried up. Them sunk ones is what fell in the dark o' the moon."

But he and Arth do not disagree about certain weather signs their mother had taught them when they were "shirt-tail boys," signs about Groundhog Day, for example, and the Ruling Days, the twelve days from the twenty-fifth of December to Old Christmas, each of which rules the weather of a month of the coming year; and how Friday is always either the fairest or the foulest day of the week; and how "there will be as many snows in the winter as there was fogs in August"; and about the equinoctial storm, and the "whippo'will storm," and the storm that wakes the frogs, and the cold spell when the dogwoods bloom, and "blackberry winter."

They like to plant their garden truck on Good Friday, if possible, because of the Easter cold spell to follow, which would be likely to nip anything already out of the ground. They are sure

[107]

that the first thunder wakes the snakes and lizards, and they know that February borrows fourteen days from March, to pay them back, in the same kind of weather, to April. Thus if the first two weeks of February are stormy the first fortnight of April will be the same.

There are stories adrift in the Cumberlands of witch haunts, haunted houses and demoniac possessions, fearsome and strange beyond any I ever heard. But Aunt Neppie Ann's modicum of common sense does not allow her to repeat them readily. She much prefers to tell of the Wild Boy who lived with the bears in the Suck fifty years ago, or of what she saw during the war, or of the few Indians she remembers. She knows, or thinks she knows, that these things are true. But she is sometimes willing to tell a certain "witch story" of a phenomenon, according to several other witnesses, actually known "up the country" where she was raised.

Perhaps every feature of this tale could be accounted for as we now account for the absurdities of New England witchcraft, by such causes as suggestion, mutual hypnotism, unconscious cerebration. The one thing not accounting for itself in this way is the perfect consistency of old Nance's character. Aunt Neppie Ann is, of course, ignorant of all literary art. Yet George Eliot herself could hardly better the picture she draws of a meddlesome, garrulous, ill-tempered old shrew who knows she has got a mean advantage over her betters and means to enjoy it to the full. Every incident, so simply related, carries new conviction. You can hear old Nance's harsh cackle of triumph, her ridicule after a successful coup directed against the preachers who would have overcome her by prayer, or the witch-doctors who would have destroyed her with silver bullets.

Nance was an old woman, or the spirit of one, and she haunted not a house, but a family, the Beavers. Her reason for bedeviling Old Leatherhead, as she called old man Beaver, was never really ascertained. Only for him, as a rule, did she set her malicious pits and snares, although sometimes she took an abrupt dislike to some visitor. So disagreeable was her nature that even those whom she called her friends would have gladly rid themselves of her presence had they been able.

At first she visited the family destined to suffer most from her, unexpectedly and at long intervals, frightening them half out of their minds on every occasion. Then she came more and more frequently, till toward the close of Beaver's days she was in the house almost all the time. Often, harried beyond endurance by her devilish pranks, Beaver would importune her to give some reason for her malice toward him.

"If I've ever done anything to wrong ye, Nance," he would say, calling her by the name she had given them, "I do wisht ye'd tell me of hit, and I'd try my best to make hit up to ye."

But the reasons she gave were contradictory, and so trivial that they satisfied no one. "You-uns plowed up my bones oncet," she was sometimes pleased to answer, or "You know you're the meanest man that ever broke the world's

[110]

bread"; and then she would go off into a fit of screeching laughter or bitter railing.

"The queerest of hit," according to Aunt Neppie Ann Lowry, "was that nobody ever seed a glimpsh of her. Bill Beaver claimed he dreamp' o' seein' her more times than a few, but nary hair o' her old head did anybody ever see with open eyes in all the years she was with 'em, though she set by 'em at the fire and done her best to make herself one o' the family. She talked might' near all the time, till she wore out their patience; she had a curi's voice, like a fly in a horn. But they never seed her.

"And yit, though you'd say she didn't have no body substance herself, she could certainly interfere and meddle with things. She could run 'em all out o' the house any minute with the foulest smells you ever heard of. She could give sich a quare taste to a fat shoat, fresh baked, that even the dogs nosed over hit and wouldn't eat a bite. She tampered with everything on the place and hid whatever was little enough so hit mout be hard to find. She'd change the noon-

[111]

mark in the door so'st Mis' Beaver wouldn't start to git dinner till way past the hour, and she'd throw ashes in the butter. Mis' Beaver hated her, if anything, a little wuss'n the old man did, bekase old Nance was always a tawmentin' the children. The next one to the baby was a real ugly-looking boy, red-headed, and ever' time he cried he spread his mouth all over his face. He had a mouth like a pore man's lease, anyhow, from year to year, and old Nance'd come down on him like a hen on a June-bug. Then Mis' Beaver had to make fair weather between 'em."

"One time the baby cried and cried in the night, keepin' the house awake, and old Nance kep' after 'em to spank hit. She said finely, 'If you-uns won't, I will,' and she did, spanked hit good. And hit shore shet up, too.

"Jist oncet in a long time hit come into her head to do somebody a good turn. Oncet when Sairy Beaver was taken down rael sick old Nance kep' the flies offen her a right smart while, and then she said: 'Sairy,' she said, 'look a-here, dawtie; I've got ye somethin' ye can eat.' And Sairy 'lowed that there was some ripe strawberries a-layin' out on the counterpin, and whur they come from she didn't know; nor likewise whur they went to, for she had no stomach to eat of 'em, and when she looked ag'in them berries was gone.

"And one time when the gals and their mother was argifyin' with a drunk man that had come in and aimed to stay, whether they wanted him or not, old man bein' away from home, old Nance she jist slapped him good and pulled him right out o' doors by the nose.

"Hit was mighty seldom she taken sich a streak, though. Mainly she was jist a meddlesome, sharp-tongued ol' critter, sich as ye meet sometimes in the flesh, and took her delight in makin' trouble night and day. She turned all pore old man Beaver's own folks ag'in him with her talk. People all over the county knowed of her and her malicious ways, and talked with her from time to time. But might' near everybody got so they didn't go to Beaverses house

[113]

much. If they had any business thar that they had got obleeged to tend to, they'd set out on the porch.

"Only the preacher he stayed there oncet overnight, and Nance she pulled the kivvers offen him, and he woke up nigh about froze.

"What? Oh, yes, they tried time and again to git shut of her, time and again. Witch-doctors couldn't phase her, and as to movin', hit was a big ondertakin'. They hadn't nary foot o' ground but that one home place. She warn't bound to the spot, anyhow. She vowed and declared she aimed to follow Old Leatherhead to the eend o' the world, till she'd vexed the life out o' his body. So they couldn't have lost her by movin', I don't reckon. . . . And she broke up every pra'ar-meetin' they tried to hold ag'in her!

" 'You old Sugarmouth!' she'd light right into the middle of a pra'ar, as apt as any way— 'you Sugarmouth, how I do love to hear ye pray and norate and go on! Not half as sweet as you was a-talkin' to Malachi's widder a-Sunday

[114]

—oh, I heared you-uns!' And everybody knowed that the preacher had sure 'nough been to Malachi's widder's house a-Sunday evening, to drive home a strayed heifer o' hern, he said. Then, 'You shet up hollerin' Amen, Noay,' she'd commence. 'How many hogs have you changed the mark on since you was at church last?' And, 'Taylor, I see you a-holdin' Sa'-Jane's hand. You wouldn't do that if Long Jim was here.' And so she'd carry on, making everything out jist nigh enough to the truth till hit couldn't be denied, yit tellin' it considerable worse'n what hit raelly was, and hittin' every feller in his weakest place, till hit look like as if the day of judgment was at hand and the secrets of all hearts revealed. There was a feller she'd called a cymblin'-headed fool that tried to act big-Ike and sass her back; sez 'e: 'Callin' your brother a fool is resky, Nance, even when ye do tell the truth.' But she started in a-tellin' somethin' nuther on him that he'd done forgot about years ago, and ag'in she got through he was more'n ready to hold his peace.

[115]

"She kep' that up till she run 'em all out, and
they heared her, as they went down the road,
cussin', whistlin', singin'—makin' fun of 'em for
everything she could think of and screechin' like
a pond full o' geese.

"Sometimes she'd go a-visitin' over-night to
see the oldest Beaver gal, that had married and
moved to Arkansas. She'd say to 'em in the
evening, 'I'm a-gwine to leave you-uns alone to-
night—for she always liked to make out that
they couldn't git along without her. 'I'm
a-gwine to Rose-Ann's,' she'd say; and they'd git
one night's rest. Then in the morning she'd be
back, tellin' 'em the news. They do tell me
that a ixpress train can't go to Arkansas and
back in that len'th o' time; yit, howsomever,
Rose-Ann's cow had the hollow-horn, or her
baby cut a tooth, or whatever. And when they
wrote to Rose-Ann's folks to find out if hit was
so hit turned out to be jist as Nance had told.

"She got meaner and meaner to pore Beaver
as he got older, until hit looked like she would
a-let up on him if she had any human mercy in

her. For he got ashamed and quare, and didn't
want to see his own neighbors that had knowed
him sence he was a little bit o' boy. He'd set
by his own ha'th and cry, and say, 'Why'n't ye
kill me, Nance, whatever ye air, and have done?'
'I will,' she'd tell him. 'I will, don't ye fret;
I'm a-gwine to.' 'Well, then,' sez 'e, 'they can
put hit on my gravestone that the wicked have
ceasted from troublin'.'

"And sure 'nough, about a month atter he
said them words they found him layin' dead in
his bed, peaceful and quiet. Some of his folks
always 'lowed that old Nance had killed him
with witchcraft."

"Do you think so, Aunt Neppie Ann?" I ask.

"I do' know. She may have, one way or another, if 'twas only by worryin' him to death."

But it seems difficult to associate the high
tragedy of murder with the spirit of a ridiculous
old crone, a spirit simply too familiar for ordinary comfort.

It is usual for the mountaineers, and, indeed,

most other men, to deny a belief in the supernatural. But, speaking for my own people, I
am sure that almost every one has had some experience he can not explain away. Perhaps he
has heard a warning of some one's death, a
strange noise, a shriek on the roof. Perhaps a
man has passed him in the open road and disappeared suddenly, leaving no tracks. Perhaps
he has been carried in a trance to strange regions
or to a great height above the earth. My people, like the Hindoos and the Scotch Highlanders, have the faculty of dealing with the occult,
of seeing and hearing that which is withheld
from more highly educated minds. Always there
is some souvenir of the spirit-world in a nook
of the mountaineer's brain. He is unwilling to
accept it, never believes quite all that it seems to
imply. Still, there it is.

CHAPTER VII

THE OLD-TIME RELIGION

"This world and one more, and then the fire-works."

THERE is preaching every third Sunday in the month at the King's Creek log church. Saturday afternoons one sees Brother Absalom Darney's pony amble down the woods-road, its rider's white hair and beard in the wind; one divines the small Bible and brass-rimmed spectacles handkerchief-swathed, and the clean shirt and change of socks in his deer-skin saddle-bags; then one tells the neighbors that "no providential hinderance" has prevented the preacher's meeting his appointment, and next morning everybody turns out to go to church.

On the first Sunday it is the same at Filmore's

Cove; on the second, at a settlement in Sequatchie; and the fourth is claimed by a for-
saken little "shack" church away back in the
Cumberland range. This is Brother Absalom's
regular circuit.

Whether any of the other charges pay him
more than King's Creek I do not know. King's
Creek has been known to give him as much as
a dollar and forty cents on one Sunday; the entire amount comes to perhaps six or eight dollars in the course of a year. Brother Ab does
not think of depending on his ministry for his
daily bread; that is earned by the sweat of his
brow, for he has a farm and a family as large as
those of the average member of his congregation. His preaching is given freely to the Lord
and His people, and neither he nor any other
mountain preacher is willing deliberately to take
up a collection for his own benefit; what comes
to him is also given freely—slipped into his hand
at the close of the service, a handful of dimes
and pennies, by whomsoever feels inclined.

Brother Ab's method of preaching is impres-

THE BAPTIZING PLACE

sively simple. There is little sensationalism about it, and still less of artifice. You hear no cant in the mountains about respect due to the cloth; our preacher is never called a clergyman or a divine; even the term "pastor and flock" savors of patronage which would indicate a false relation; Brother So-and-So, preacher of the gospel, is title enough. He is not of a class set apart from life, from the labors, sins and sorrows of his world, nor does he pander to any class distinction. He is as incapable of kowtowing to the highest as of condescension to the meanest. Whatever his inconsistencies, whatever his ignorance, whatever the narrowness of his outlook on Scripture and theology—and these failings are sure to be many, for no amount of education ever quite rids the mountaineer of bullheaded contrariness—he is certain to be, first of all, sincere, a man among men, fearlessly expounding the gospel as he knows it.

The popular opinion about Brother Absalom seems to be that, while he is of little value in raising revivals, he offers nothing but strong

Scriptural meat without false doctrine. I can well believe that he presents no false doctrine, for, so far as I have heard, he tries to steer clear of doctrinal subjects altogether—close communion, the apostolic succession, free will, original sin, and all the other questions over which the mountain people are so fond of splitting hairs.

The time of "taking up church" is uncertain. After a sufficient congregation has assembled, according to the preacher's judgment, he and some of the amen-corner members raise a hymn, which serves instead of a bell to concentrate the gathering. They sing without books, for these hymns have never been printed: "They'll pray for me," "We have mothers up in heaven," "Father's gone to glory," and a hundred like them. As other voices take up the strain (it is not etiquette to join in until the recognized leaders have sung the first stanza) the people gossiping outside begin to take their seats, whole families clambering out of hay-bedded wagons, the women folk clucking decorously all the way to the door and stopping every five steps to settle the plumage of their broods; old fellows, half-hunter, half farmer, choosing a place on the left, well forward; young wives and maids, modest without primness, sweet without coquetry; lean boys with a promise of strong beauty in their faces, sliding in warily and never venturing far from the open door; and a host of perfectly grave children of all ages. Some of the men are careful to place themselves near a window (for of late four little square-paned windows have been added to the old log house, which seems from the road to wear an expression of astonishment in consequence), so as to keep an eye on their horses hitched in the woods outside. But Brother Absalom, who himself has ridden a rather freakish pony, displays no concern for any but the work in hand. After the singing he rises in his place behind the square desk of shelves that serves for pulpit, combing his grand beard with his fingers, and thoughtfully, weightily, reads a chapter. Then he asks the congregation to kneel with him in prayer, with a slight emphasis that destroys the conventionality of the

[123]

phrase and brings as many as possible actually
to their knees; for he makes a point of teaching
simplicity and humility in all his churches.

Another hymn is sung, maybe two or three—
droned through, a disciple of Moody and San-
key would say, although these people really sing
for sheer enjoyment—and then Brother Absalom announces his text. The last sermon I heard
him preach had for its subject "Prayer." He began: "There are two thoughts in this text. One
is that God is always to be reached by prayer."
And he plunged abruptly into his sermon, which
from beginning to end was a mere stringing together of tales abridged from the very words of
the Book. The prayer of David, the prayer of
Daniel, the prayer of the Pharisee and the pub-
lican, the prayer in Gethsemane—he recounted
them all, and several others, quite simply, com-
mencing each story with "We are told," and
often ending with a sort of moral in his own
words, addressed pointedly to some one near
him: "That, Brother Jim, is the kind of prayer
that God Almighty loves to hear."

[124]

This informality, this direct simplicity, is the strength of Brother Absalom's sermons. At first the babies fretted with the heat; some refused to be comforted, and had to be carried into the open air; a young mother grew more and more embarrassed over her efforts to quiet the delicate-looking little whimperer in her arms, and presently the preacher interrupted himself to say: "Don't let yourselves get troubled about them little folks makin' a noise! I'm well used to that; hit don't disturb me none, and won't disturb nobody else that really wants to listen at the gospel." He added some remarks about the child having the best right in the house of God that were really beautiful and touching, and dismissed the subject by saying that they would all go to sleep in a short time. And they did. I must say that the strained, slightly nasal pitch of a mountain preacher's voice, and its cadence, rather like an energetic chant, is well calculated to put any one to sleep; there is more than a little mesmerism about it.

Returning to his text, our preacher said that

the second part of it had to do with vows and obligations, and explained what he understood to be the nature of a vow. Here again followed a disconnected series of anecdotes: Jepthah's vow and Jonah's, with the simpler morals to be derived from each. Like other mountain preachers, he speaks readily on his feet without preparation, scarcely once opening a book of which he can repeat whole pages by heart. He told, too, the story of Zaccheus, making much of his promise to "restore fourfold," and I think that was all.

He ended with an appeal to the sinners to come forward and be prayed for. Six or eight responded, some half hypnotized, others battling, manfully and visibly, with self-consciousness; they gave the preacher their hands, while the congregation sang:

"I will arise and go to Jesus,
    He will embrace me in His arms;
In the arms of my dear Saviour,
    Oh, there are ten thousand charms."

[126]

After prayer, in which all the leading men of the church joined—all praying at once at the top of their voices, or at least ejaculating "Lord grant it" from time to time—the "right hand of Christian fellowship" was called for. The ceremony is frankly a general hand-shaking and a hearty song; it promotes good feeling, and signifies little else. "Let all who hope to meet me in the Promised Land give me their hands."

"Oh, fathers, will you meet me,
Say, fathers, will you meet me,
Say, fathers, will you meet me,
On Canaan's happy shore?"

"By the grace of God I'll meet you,
By the grace of God I'll meet you,
By the grace of God I'll meet you,
On Canaan's happy shore."

The next verse is precisely the same, except that it is addressed to the "mothers" instead of "fathers"; the third verse is to "brothers"; the rest of the succession runs to sisters, Christians, neighbors, mourners, and finally preachers. Many of the hymns are constructed on this plan —perhaps only to save trouble in composition, although it is certain that repetition has its effect on these excited, outwearied brains. The preacher's voice strikes through the words of the song with encouraging shouts of goodwill; the singers throng and press about him on the floor, grasping hands right and left—for it is a fact that under the religious spell even the inveterate shyness of the young people vanishes like a dry leaf in flames. Tears are running down seamed and withered faces now, as the repression and loneliness of many months find relief; the tune changes again, and yet again—they do not tire of this.

"I hope to meet the fathers there,
I hope to meet the fathers there,
I hope to meet the fathers there,
And play on the golden harps.
I hope to meet the mothers there——"

[128]

Broken ties restored, old pain of lonely nights to be no more—that is the dearest promise of this religion; the aching of old grief is suddenly caught up and whirled away in this aroused hope of glory.

"By-and-by we'll go and see them,
By-and-by we'll go and see them,
By-and-by we'll go and see them,
   On the other bright shore.
That bright day may be to-morrow,
That bright day may be to-morrow——"

Did ever Israel captive peer into the future any more wistfully than these?

"Glory to God, my soul's happy!" It is a woman's scream that rings high over all. Several break into sobbing; the woman throws herself down with her head and arms across a bench. One touches her in friendly fashion; the rest sing on:

"Hit's the old-time religion,
Hit's the old-time religion,

[129]

Hit's the old-time religion,
  And hit's good enough for me,
    Good enough for me;
Hit was good for our fathers,
  And hit's good enough for me."

At last the wave of emotion spends itself; the handshaking is over. A few more songs and they are ready to go home, after Brother Absalom's benediction.

Now, here is religious teaching of no literary quality whatever; sermons by an ignorant man, a man who probably does not regard a high degree of education as a desirable or even a right thing. It is generally denied that good can come of such teaching. The blind cannot lead the blind, and from the outsider's point of view the ways of these people are ludicrous in the extreme. But that is if one does not understand.

Aside from religious precept, from the moral tone of the teaching—aside, too, from example, if one admits that all this veneration for things held sacred, no matter what, has its effect on the

[130]

young and the uncontrolled—aside from these things, which are more or less to be taken for granted, there is yet to be considered a feature not usually thought of. I mean the break in the loneliness of their lives, the meeting for once on a footing which is both decorous and friendly, of those who at almost any other time are isolated even more by peculiarity of temperament than by the distance between their homes. What going to church really means to a woman who during the rest of the month sees hardly a face outside her family is difficult to realize—a woman, say, like that poor widow Electa Fetridge. She is known to subsist, with her children, on white beans, hoecake and scant portions of bulk pork from week's end to week's end, and has no more mental endowment than is necessary to enable her to mourn for a husband who drank himself to death some years ago. Yet amid the competition for the preacher's society that arose immediately after the benediction Brother Darney made answer to the husband of more than one excellent cook: "No, thank you, brother;

I'd like the best in the world to see you and your folks, but I've done promised to go home with Sister 'Lectar Fetridge."

This was only an ordinary day-meeting, when men's thoughts must necessarily be distracted by their own affairs—their horses, their dinners waiting at home. Far more exciting is a revival, "a big meetin'," held night after night as long as the interest continues; far more picturesque the "brush meetings," held in some charming nook of the woods; far more beautiful the baptizings. Nothing I have ever seen in the ritual of any religion has seemed to me more lovely and impressive than the ceremonies of baptism and foot-washing as here conducted. Baptism could hardly have been simpler as taught by the early Apostles themselves. The place is a clear pool fringed with ferns; at its up-creek end a little fall flashes over a gray ledge of rock, breaking the silence of deep woods with its clear, sudden clamor. Here, once or twice in a twelve-month—usually at the close of a revival, or, as we say, "when big meetin' breaks"—the new converts are baptized. All their kin come with them for encouragement, and such of the countryside as are not kin come for the spectacle. The season is not considered, nor the state of one's health; I have known persons in very feeble condition to be dipped into these cold spring-fed streams without sustaining the least injury, and it is nothing uncommon for women and children to be baptized through the ice. They say no one is ever made ill by the performance of a religious duty; certainly there is a plenty of violent exercise connected with this one. Most of the converts are shouting by the time they gain the bank, and nearly run amuck in the crowd before they can be persuaded to retire to a hastily erected brush shelter and change to dry clothing.

No attempt is ever made to check the excitement, although its excess has been known to result in insanity and even death, for whoso dies shouting happy is held to have met a fortunate end. I hesitate to say much of this, for there is a tendency among certain classes of city people to make a jest of these peculiarities, to which we

[133]

of the mountains are becoming more sensitive year by year. It ought not to be so—God knows what the old ceremonies mean to those who take part in them; but such is the persecution in some places where the curiosity of the town is pressing close in on us that even after a congregation has met together to hold a foot-washing, if any city people are present who are not well known and trusted, the occasion will be quietly turned into an ordinary preaching. It requires considerable courage in men, and especially in women, to go through with this primitive ceremony in the face of unsympathetic onlookers.

One afternoon a group of "natives" in the blacksmith shop were contentedly chewing tobacco and swapping remarks at long intervals. Unexpectedly a stripling of the summer people broke into the trickle of talk with: "Oh, say, is there going to be any shouting next Sunday? 'Cause our crowd is going up if there is."

For a minute it seemed the others had not heard—certainly one would never have suspected their hatred of that boy. Then one

[134]

drawled, easily: "I don't know; there wasn't any give out at meetin' last Sunday." And they all chewed on like so many oxen.

It takes a brave man, for that matter, to believe what the mountaineer believes, let alone to uphold it in the face of ridicule. Is it always courage—or is it sometimes contrariness? One cannot be sure. A "doctrinal sermon" is certain to arouse bitter dissension in any church; yet the people are fond of such, and exult openly in their excellent powers of disputation.

The shortest and hottest debate I ever witnessed was one that took place just outside the church door between a fledgling preacher and the oldest woman of the neighborhood. The young fellow had just delivered a sermon on the apostolic succession, declaring that no one could possibly be saved without baptism at the hands of a preacher of his own particular denomination; he had even named his mother—with respect and with deep regret, it is true, but still he mentioned her—as one he believed to be among the eternally lost on account of this fail-

[135]

ure to comply with Scriptural injunction. Outside the door, after meeting, an old woman faced him, trembling with indignation.

"Lishy," she shrilled at him, unheeding the crowd, "Lishy Robbins, I held you in my arms before you was three hours old, and I cert'ny never 'lowed to see you stand up in a church and preach as you've been a-preachin' this day! Lishy Robbins, me and your mother was girls together; I knowed her all her life, and when she died nobody grieved for her any more than I did. There never was a better woman or a better Christian in any church, and if she hain't in heaven today——" The old voice broke; she gathered herself together and went close to the lad. "Lishy Robbins, you ought to be slapped over for preachin' any such foolishness about your mother, and I'm a-gwine to do it!"

And forthwith she did. Her toil-hardened old fist shot out so unexpectedly that the young preacher went down like a cornstalk. Angry? Of course he was angry, but she was a grandmother of the mountains. There was nothing

[136]

for it but to pick himself up with as much dignity as remained to him; and now that after-years of experience have somewhat mellowed his headstrong humors, he is wont to tell that good story on himself as heartily as if he had ceased to believe in the apostolic succession.

But we never let go of a belief once fixed in our minds. A sort of home missionary of culture once spent two hours explaining the motions of the earth to the King's Creek men, with the aid of a good globe and a lantern to represent the sun. They hearkened to him gravely, with the most respectful attention, being won by his evident sincerity and goodwill; but the "four corners of the earth" and Joshua's command to the sun and moon were in their minds all the time, I am sure. Not one was budged a hair's-breadth from his original opinion.

Nothing would be easier than to show, by quoting the language of sermons, experience meetings and "talk meetings," exactly what the mountaineer thinks is his religion; but this language is so much a matter of rote that it is

[137]

widely misleading. The thing a man honestly supposes himself to believe—that is to say, the creed he subscribes to, the religion he carries to church with him—and the things he does unconsciously believe and rely upon, heart and soul, are apt to be two different matters in any case. And it is especially so with folks so little given to retrospection that they can hardly discover what are their own inmost thoughts, much less give them expression.

In a settlement in our mountains one may find Missionary Baptists, Hardshell Baptists, Cumberlands, Calvinists, and what not; but at the bottom they are very much the same. Arguments frequently arise and become bitter over questions of immersion, close communion, original sin and the like; but the principles that control their daily habit of mind, the beliefs that are the mainsprings of thought and action, do not differ nearly so much between man and man as the propounders of doctrines would have us suppose. One mountaineer may believe that negroes are descended from some animal resembling a monkey; his neighbor may "see by the Scripture" that it is not only improper for a woman to speak in church, but that she must under no circumstances remove her sunbonnet during religious service; another's favorite crotchet may be his conviction that the earth is supported floating on an infinite expanse of water; while yet a fourth declares "once in grace always in grace," and will argue the subject all day Sunday. Each one produces abundance of Scripture texts to fortify his position, and over these matters they constantly disagree; yet, although no amount of talking will make them admit it, their attitude toward the supernatural world is really the same.

To talk of these first principles rather than of creeds is a harder and far more important task; whether a man "believes in" ghosts or no is a small matter, and whether he practice foot-washing or no is a still lesser thing. But whether he looks into his world and sees there a law and order beyond human power, and whether he lends himself to the order or sets himself against it—this is surely the mightiest import of his existence.

Courage seems to me the keynote of our whole system of religious thought. The fatalism of this free folk is unlike anything of the Far East; dark and mystical though it be through much brooding over the problem of evil, it is lighted with flashes of the spirit of the Vikings. A man born and bred in a vast wild land nearly always becomes a fatalist. He learns to see Nature not as a thing of fields and brooks, friendly to man and docile beneath his hand, but as a world of depths and heights and distances illimitable, of which he is but a tiny part. He feels himself carried in the sweep of forces too vast for comprehension, forces variously at war, out of which are the issues of life and death, but in which the Order, the Right, must certainly prevail. This is the beginning of his faith as he had it from his fathers; from hence is his courage and his independence. Inevitably he comes to feel, with a sort of proud humility, that he has no part or lot in the control of the universe save as he allies

[140]

himself, by prayer and obedience, with the Order that rules.

Hence this is to him the whole value of prayer: his wrestlings with the spirit are all undertaken with a view to placing himself in the right attitude; his prayers are almost never mere requests to be granted; he will not cheapen his religion to a scheme for getting what he wants. The conversion of a near friend or a relative is often prayed for especially, and sometimes the recovery of one sick unto death, "if it be Thy will"; but one of my people would never think of praying, for instance, for rain. I have known a starving widow to pray for bread, and once an old herb doctor to pray for light on a case of hemorrhage he didn't understand; the widow bestirred herself to seek, and was, of course, fed by her neighbors, while the doctor claims to have received a special revelation anent the application of red clay, and the result gave doctor and patient much satisfaction. But, with a few exceptions of this sort, it is not customary to pray for temporal benefits at all.

Implicit faith in every word contained in the Bible, whether it were uttered by the prophets, added by King James' translators or inserted as explanatory by the compiler of the Concordance, is too pathetic to be amusing. A lad arrested last year for voting under age put forward as his defense, in all good faith, the fact that the date of his birth, which showed him twenty-one, though he was proved to be younger, had been scrawled on the flyleaf of his Testament ever since he could remember. He knew it was so, he declared, because his Bible told him so. It was impossible that an error should exist between its revered covers.

There is no telling what conclusions one of our mountain people may draw from a given portion of Scripture. His religion is really the outgrowth of his own nature and environment rather than of the written Word—although he would, of course, indignantly deny that such is the case. He believes that he reads the Book and conducts himself according to its tenets to the best of his ability; but he is most of the time reading himself into the Bible. And many are those of far superior intelligence who read in the same way as unconsciously as the mountaineer. "You can't foretell nothing in this world certainly," said a hard-headed man to a valley preacher who was arguing certain prophecies of his own. "Didn't Christ refuse to give them Pharisees a sign? Didn't He tell 'em, 'Ye say when ye see the sky red at morning,' and so on? —I fergit the words, but He never even told 'em a red sunrise meant rain; He told 'em, *'Ye say'* thus and so. *He knowed the weather does just as hit pleases!"*

What is to be will be. So consistently do they hold to this that they hardly permit themselves the habit of casual wishing; an almost passionate pride of independence prevents their yielding to vain longings, far enough, at least, to give them voice. "I desire an interest in all your pra'ars, and hope I may hold out faithful to the end," and "I want to get a home in heaven," are favorite formulas for the closing of these intensely earnest, mystical "experiences" recounted at

[143]

meeting; but I have suspected that they would as lief add "Yours truly," if it were as customary a phrase. Certainly these are almost the only wishes one ever hears expressed.

Such is our religion in the mountains; a religion in which the narrowest creeds and the broadest hearty human fellowship are oddly at variance; a religion stripped of artificiality at the cost of parting with its conventions of beauty and grace. The mountaineer will have none of the thousand and one adjuncts of modern forms of worship lest they obscure his vision of vital truth; the light of the Spirit, he believes, should shine as sunlight does, its primordial life-giving splendor undimmed by arts of stained glass and embroidery. It is for this reason that he chooses one of the more primitive denominations— Methodist, Baptist, Campbellite, Cumberland— and abides by its dogmas to the end of his days. Man to man, simply and forcibly, our preachers must and will speak, "converting" by personal influence as naturally as healers employ the human touch. If he makes himself ridiculous, as might often seem to more sophisticated view; if he forbids his congregation the use of instrumental music or the wearing of jewelry; if he cries down all graces of refinement—one must bear in mind that it is because of a real passion for simplicity; it is not the mere blundering crudeness of a boor.

CHAPTER VIII

SOME REAL AMERICAN MUSIC

IT is generally believed that America has no
folk-music, nothing distinctively native out
of which a national school of advanced composition may arise. The commercial spirit of the
age and our conventional mode of existence have
so far effaced original types of character and
romantic phases of life that the folk-song seems
already a thing of the past.

Dvorak and a few other composers have indeed made use of negro themes, and the aboriginal Indian music has been seriously treated more
than once. But these compositions, however excellent, are no expression of American life and
character. They fall as strangely on our ears
as any foreign product.

But here, among the mountains of Kentucky,

[146]

GOIN' UP CRIPPLE CREEK

Tennessee and the Carolinas, is a people of whose inner nature and its musical expression almost nothing has been said. The music of the Southern mountaineer is not only peculiar, but, like himself, peculiarly American.

Nearly all mountaineers are singers. Their untrained voices are of good timbre, the women's being sweet and high and tremulous, and their sense of pitch and tone and rhythm remarkably true. The fiddler and the banjo-player are well treated and beloved among them, like the minstrels of feudal days.

The mountain fiddler rarely cuddles his instrument under his chin. He sets it against the middle of his chest, and grasping his bow near the middle wields it with a jiggling movement quite unlike the long sweep of the accomplished violinist's bow-arm. One might complain that their playing is too rapid and jerky. But all the dance-tunes, at least, are composed for this tempo, and no other would be found suitable.

The music, while usually minor, is not of a plaintive tendency. There are few laments, no sobbing and wailing. In this it differs radically from that of savage peoples. Neither has it any martial throb and clang. It is reflective, meditative; the tunes chuckle, not merrily, but in amused contemplation.

The mountaineer is fond of turning the joke on himself. He makes fun of his own poverty, his own shiftlessness, his ignorance, his hard luck and his crimes.

I'll tune up my fid - dle and ros - in my bow, And make my - self wel - come wher - ev - er I go.

I'll buy my own whiskey and make my own stew;
If it does make me drunk it is nothing to you.

I'll eat when I'm hungry and drink when I'm
        dry;
If a tree don't fall on me, I'll live till I die.

[148]

BLIND COON DOG.

I went up on the mountain, once, And
give my horn a blow, And ev-'ry gal in the
val-ley Come a-run-ning to the do'.

There's some that like the fat of the meat,
   And some that like the lean,
But they that have no cake to bake
   Can keep their kitchen clean.

As I went down to my old field I heard a mighty
     maulin';
The seed-ticks was a-splittin' rails, the chiggers
     was a-haulin'.

Once touched by religious emotion, however,
the mountaineer seems to lose his sense of the
ridiculous entirely. The deeps of his nature are
reached at last. The metaphors of Scripture,
the natural expression of the Oriental mind, are

[149]

taken with a literalness and seriousness against which one cannot help thinking a touch of humor might be a saving grace.

Hit's the old Ship of Zion, as she comes,
Hit's the old Ship of Zion, as she comes,
Hit's the old Ship of Zion, the old Ship of Zion,
Hit's the old Ship of Zion as she comes.

She'll be loaded with bright angels when she
    comes, etc.

I see her flag a-wavin' as she comes, etc.

Oh, brothers, what will you do when she comes,
    etc.

We will flee to the rocks and the mountains, etc.

Repetition carried to the point of wearisomeness is a favorite form of revival hymns. It seems to be a necessary feature, similar to the monotonous beating of the West Indians' bamboula that incites their savage minds to frenzy.

Some have fathers up in glory,
Some have fathers up in glory,
Some have fathers up in glory,
    On the other bright shore.

I be-lieve in be-ing read-y,

I be-lieve in be-ing read-y,

I be-lieve in be-ing read-y,

When this world's at an end.

Some bright day we'll go and see them,
Some bright day we'll go and see them,
Some bright day we'll go and see them,
    On the other bright shore.

That bright day may be to-morrow, etc.

Some have mothers up in glory, etc.

[151]

Oh, just let me in the kingdom,
Oh, just let me in the kingdom,
Oh, just let me in the kingdom,
When this world's at an end.

RAIN, MIGHTY LORD.

Rain, oh, rain, mighty Sav - - iour,

Rain con - vert - ing pow - er down,

Rain, might - y Lord. The way the ho - ly

proph - ets went, Rain, might - y

Sav - iour, The road that leads from

ban - ish - ment, Rain, might - y Lord.

[152]

Here a feeling for the supernatural sets in. The oddly changing keys, the endings that leave the ear in expectation of something to follow, the quavers and falsettos, become in recurrence a haunting hint of the spirit-world; neither beneficent nor maleficent, neither devil nor angel, but something—something not to be understood, yet to be certainly apprehended. It is to the singer as if he stood within a sorcerer's circle, crowded upon by an invisible throng.

Shout, shout, we're gaining ground,
 O halle-hallelujah;
The power of God is a-comin' down—
 O glory hallelu'.

I do believe beyond a doubt,
 O halle-hallelujah;
The Christian has a right to shout—
 O glory hallelu'.

It is their one emotional outlet. Having no theatre, no bull-fight, no arena, no sensational feature of any kind in their lives, they must,

[153]

being a high-strung race, find vent some other way.

They rock to and fro, softly crooning and moaning through song and prayer, until the impulse comes upon them to leap into the air and scream and shout until exhausted. It is common for women and even strong men to injure themselves unawares; or, at baptizings, to pitch headlong into the water. I have seen convulsions and even temporary insanity brought on by these excesses. It is partly the music that induces this mental state. But these songs cannot be fairly judged sung out of their natural setting of brushwood camp or half-lighted log church, and reinforced by the vibrant, hurried voices of exhorters and the high strained singsong of the preacher who has reached what is known as his "weavin' way." I confess that the wild fascination of a mountain revival has a strange power over me. The scene and the music draw me with a charm that I do not understand.

Such a religion has little to do with the moral

[154]

law. I am far from wishing to imply that they regard no principles of right and wrong, or that their own peculiar code of morals is not rigidly adhered to by the majority; of this I have spoken elsewhere in this book. But, like most primitive peoples, they are prone to hold brute courage the first of the virtues, and the hero of their ballad is too often the criminal. The bold robber stands to their minds as the buccaneers and marooners of the Spanish Main stood to seventeenth-century England. He is the Man Who Dared, that is all, and if he be overtaken by justice, their sympathies, of course, follow him all the more.

Last night as I lay sleeping I dreamt a pleasant
    dream:
I dreamt I was down in Moscow, 'way down by
    Pearly stream;
The prettiest girl beside me had come to go my
    bail;
I woke up, broken-hearted, in Knoxville county
    jail.

[155]

In come my jailer, about nine o'clock,
A bunch of keys was in his hand, my cell-door
    to unlock,
Saying, "Cheer you up, my prisoner, for I heard
    some voices say
You're bound to hear your sentence some time
    to-day."

In come my mother, about ten o'clock,
Saying, "Oh, my lovin' Johnny, what sentence
    have you got?"
"The jury's found me guilty, and the judge,
    a-standin' by,
Has sent me down to Knoxville, to lock me up
    to die."

THE GAMBLING MAN.

My daddy was a gambler,
  He learned me how to play;
He told me I should always stand
  On the ace-jack-deuce-and-trey.

My mammy used to talk to me
  Of things I hadn't seen;

[156]

Said she, "My boy, you'll be in the workhouse
Before you are sixteen."

I knew she was a-talkin',
But I thought she was in fun,
But I had to wear the ball and chain
Before I was twenty-one.

I'll play cards with any white man,
And I'll play with him fair;
I'll play the hat right off his head,
And I'll play him for his hair.

I've gambled away my pocketbook,
I've gambled away my comb,
I've gambled away all the money I had
And now I will go home.

There are simple dance tunes, with a rollick-
ing banjo accompaniment, such as "Citico,"
"Shady Grove" and "Muskrat," to which a
shuffling step is measured, the couples dancing
in an "eight-handed set."

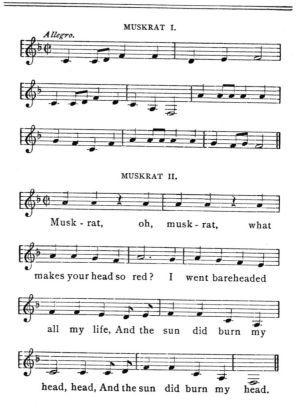

Romantic love as a *motif* is almost altogether absent throughout the mountaineer's music. It is a subject of which he is very shy. His passion is

[158]

not a thing to be proclaimed from the housetops. Once married, his affection is a beautiful thing, faithful to whatever end. But he does not sing of it.

The young men and maidens have, however, something that stands to them instead of love songs—almost, one suspects, instead of wooing. These are the "kissing games," half dance, half romping child-play. They are next of kin to the old May-pole dance, real playing at love—games in which much choosing of partners takes place, and many kisses are taken openly, in wholesome lightness of heart, as part of the game. These are such games as the children of more civilized societies play. But the children of the log church school rarely organize their frolics into games. Their sport is scarcely more elaborate than the romping of colts in a pasture, or the imitative pranks of monkeys. They are half-grown lads and girls who sing these songs, and tall bachelors are not in the least ashamed of joining in with whole-hearted abandon.

[159]

Hit's over the river to feed my sheep,
Hit's over the river, Charley;
Hit's over the river to feed my sheep,
And see my lonesome darling.

You stole my partner, to my dislike,
You stole my partner, to my dislike,
You stole my partner, to my dislike,
And also my dear darling.

I'll have her back before daylight,
(And so forth.)

The following is a game of marriage, with a
ceremony of joining hands:

All around the ring so straight,
Go choose the one to be your mate.

After the choosing a shout of derision goes
up:

Law, law, law, what a choice you've made!
Better in the grave you had a-been laid.

But after all, when the ceremony is completed, they are ready to dance round the happy pair:

Kiss the bride, and kiss her sweet;
Now you rise upon your feet.

Another contains a description of a burlesque paradise:

Where coffee grows on white-oak trees,
    The river runs with brandy,
The boys are made of lumps of gold,
    And the girls are sweet as candy.

"Weevily Wheat" is very old and very popular. It is more like a dance than a game:

O law, mother, my toes are sore,
    Tra la la la la la la;
Dancing on your sandy floor,
    Tra la la la la la;
Your weevily wheat isn't fit to eat,
    And neither is your barley;
I won't have none of your weevily wheat
    To make a cake for Charley.

[161]

Charley he is a handsome lad,
  Charley he is a dandy;
Charley he is the very one
  That sold his hat for brandy.
Your weevily wheat isn't fit to eat,
  And neither is your barley;
We'll have some flour in half an hour
  To make a cake for Charley.

It is not improbable that the "Charley" of these songs is the Prince Charlie of Jacobite ballads. "Over the River, Charley," may or may not be an echo of "Over the Waters to Charlie," for a large proportion of the mountain people are descended from Scotch Highlanders who left their homes on account of the persecutions which harassed them during Prince Charlie's time and began life anew in the wilderness of the Alleghenies.

Be that as it may, the mountain people do sing many ballads of old England and Scotland. Their taste in music has no doubt been guided by these, which have come down from their ancestors. Indeed, so closely do they keep to the musical tradition of the ballad form that it is often difficult to distinguish the old from their own more modern compositions, especially as some have been recast, words, names of localities and obsolete or unfamiliar phrases having been changed to fit their comprehension—Chester town being substituted for London town, and the like. It should delight the heart of the student of English to compare the following instance with "The Clerk's Twa Sons of Owsenford" and "The Wife of Usher's Well":

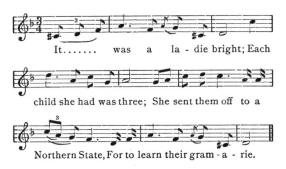

It....... was a la - die bright; Each
child she had was three; She sent them off to a
Northern State, For to learn their gram - a - rie.

They had been gone but a little time—
Two months, perhaps, or three—
Till sickness spread all over that land
And swept her babes away.

She prayed if there was a King in heaven
Who chose to wear a crown,
That He would send them home that night,
Or in the morning soon.

'Twas twelve long months, about Christmas
time,
The night being cold and long,
The three little ones came running home
And into their mother's arms.

She set a table before them soon,
On it spread bread and wine.
"Now, come along, my little babes,
Come, eat and drink of mine."
"I may not eat of your bread, mother,
Nor drink none of your wine."

She fixed a bed in the back room side,
On it spread a clean sheet,

And over the top spread a golden skirt,
For to make a sweeter sleep.

"Awake, awake," said the eldest one,
"Now soon the cock will crow;
I see our Saviour smiling down,
And to Him we must go.

"Cold clods of clay lie over our heads,
Green grass grows at our feet;
You've shed tears enough for me, mother,
For to wet a winding-sheet."

Some of the best instrumental music is of a
descriptive nature, reflecting vividly the inci-
dents of every-day life. Peculiar fingerings of
the strings, close harmonies, curious snaps and
slides and twangs, and the accurate observations
of an ear attuned to all the sounds of nature
enter into the composition of these. In the
"Cackling Hen" the cackle, hard, high and
cheerfully prosaic, is very well rendered, as may
be easily seen:

CACKLING HEN.

"Big Jim" is a dance tune in which the major melody drops suddenly into a running repetition of two or three minor notes, beautifully like the drumming of rain on a cabin roof.

In "The Fox Chase" the baying of the hounds, from the eager start of the pack as they take up the trail to the last lingering yelp after the quarry is treed, is given by the banjo accompaniment. The spoken "patter" runs along irrespective of rhythm, interpolated regularly with the hunting cry. It is almost impossible to re-

[166]

duce the effect to musical notation. The emphasis is all on the hounds' deep note; and the
thumb-string, while almost imperceptible to the
ear, still plays an important part in producing
the rhythm. It begins with a regular movement
which grows more and more rapid and exciting

THE FOX–CHASE.

as it progresses. Then, as the fox is treed, the close comes, suddenly, with the baying of "Old Sounder."

Boys, blow up the dogs and let's have a fox-chase. Get the horn and give her a toot. Call up the dogs and we'll go down on the creek. *Whoopee!* Go it, Lead!

Come on, boys, and let's go down on the point of the ridge and hear this fox-chase. They will fetch him out on the other side. *Whoopee!* Go it, Lead! Come on, old dog! *Whoopee!*

Just listen at those dogs run that fox! Listen, boys! I believe they have run him down in the gulf; we can just hear them down in there. *Whoopee!* Go it, Lead!

Just listen at 'em, boys! They have started him out of the creek. *Whoopee!* Come on, old dogs!

Come, boys, let's go round on the point of the

ridge and hear that race. *Whoopee!* Just listen at Old Sounder!

Boys, they are bringing him out on the ridge. Just hear old Lead—Bow! bow! wow! wow!

Come on, boys; you will miss the best part of the race. *Whoopee!* Hold 'em down, Rocks!

Boys, I can't stay here any longer—I've got to go to those dogs. I believe I hear old Lead at that old tree—bow, wow, wow! Let's go to them—they are treed on Round Knob. *Whoopee!* Coming to you, old dogs!

As I write these songs old memories come drifting on their melody—memories of drowsy noons and the tankle-tump-a-tankle of the banjo on the porch, and the thump-chug, thump-chug of the batten as the mother's shuttle went patiently to and fro; of yodels ringing down the gulch; of spinning-wheel songs—old Scotch ballads blurred together with the crescendo and

[169]

diminuendo of the whirling spokes; of the crooning "By-ee . . . By-ee . . ." that lulls little children to sleep; of the laugh and leap of dancers bounding through Cripple Creek at the bidding of a man told off to call the figures; of red firelight flickering over an impromptu play-party, neighbor lads and girls singing and romping through all the evolutions of those intricate games of courtship in which the couples are never finally mated, saluting and pirouetting and following and flouting; of wilder nights at "big meetin'," when, an awed and fascinated child, I clung to the wall or clambered on the puncheon benches to be out of harm's way; of the ripple of water and the drone of bees . . .

Had I but words to say how these tunes are bound with the life of the singer, knit with his earliest sense-impressions, and therefore dearer than any other music could ever be—impossible to forget as the sound of his mother's voice!

Crude with a tang of the Indian wilderness, strong with the strength of the mountains, yet, in a way, mellowed with the flavor of Chaucer's

[170]

time—surely this is folk-song of a high order. May it not one day give birth to a music that shall take a high place among the world's great schools of expression?

CHAPTER IX

THE LITERATURE OF A WOLF-RACE

AS with our music, so with our literature. It is surprising that there should remain, so near, comparatively, to centers of civilization, a people with a literature of their own as yet untouched by student or story-writer. I do not refer to studies in the dialect by authors such as John Fox and Miss Murfree, but the compositions of the mountaineers themselves, in song and proverb and story, made for no other public than their own circle. Of course, it is all purely oral, for very few of the mountain people can read and write. But it is literature, for all that.

A word first as to the vernacular.

Among all the varieties of English spoken in this polyglot country, whose every separate State has set its mark on the mother-tongue, there is,

[172]

I believe, not one which possesses a true literary value, unless it be the speech of the mountaineers. This, while perhaps not equal to the Scotch as used by Burns in the composition of some of his most touching poems, is yet a genuine dialect, to be distinguished from mere barbarism and corruption. Most native tongues now spoken in the United States are either forms corrupted from standard English or bastard forms arising from a mixture with some other language, as French-English, Mexican-English, negro-English. There are numerous instances of pure obsolete usage in the famous New England dialect. But it does not compare in this respect with that of the mountains, many of whose word-forms are historic, and only to be found, in literature, in works antedating the close of the sixteenth century.

This dialect is, of course, sprinkled thickly with corruptions. There is probably no authority whatever for "you-uns,"and examples might be multiplied indefinitely to show the degradation of English in the mouth of the mountaineer.

[173]

But, even so, there is enough excellent Saxon and Gaelic left to prove the right of the dialect to a place of honor. Homely as it is, one gains here an idea of the old unpolluted language of the English people as Macaulay loved it, "rich in its own proper wealth, little improved by all that it has borrowed" since Chaucer's day: simple, sincere, full of the energy of forcible Saxon words; unexcelled in clearness, spirit and strength. I think that I personally obtain a peculiar pleasure from the reading of old authors not granted to many, from so familiar knowledge of the old form in which they wrote. I am enabled to read more as their own contemporary public may have read them.

When my neighbor hails me, as I ride by his door, with an invitation to "light and hitch," I am reminded of the boy's exclamation in Julius Cæsar, as he watches the horsemen on the plain:

"Now some light. O, he lights, too."

When Gran'ma sends over to borrow a "race

o' brimstone" it recalls a passage in Twelfth Night about "a race or two of ginger." Not even the dictionary explains, as Gran'ma might, that a race is a little stick, a bar. And the "boogar" that scares the baby, is he not next of kin to the Irish pooka, as well as to bogey and spook? You meet him in Spenser, and also in a certain old version of the Bible which says, "Thou shalt not be afeared of any bugges by night."

There seems to me a taste of staleness and tameness in the speech of civilized people. Of course, I am not thinking of the master who uses the language as a fine instrument, evoking harmonies of word and thought. The ordinary intercourse of men in city and country is a language sapped, by conventional habit and usage, of its most vital qualities.

There is a certain wild and elemental poetry in the speech of the mountaineer, the "bow-arrow tang" that Thoreau loved. He is never quite commonplace, for all his uncouth exterior. There is a rude instinct—not even barbaric, but

[175]

drawn straight from the fountains of the nature about him, to flow, dark but living, through his own, that, though ever so crude and sour and embryonic a thing, mixing itself with ludicrous awkwardness more often than not, yet sometimes finds the right word unerringly. He says exactly what he means to say, and says it pungently. When he refers to the population of a particular cove or bend as an "acorn-fed tribe," does not the epithet paint you a picture of starvelings herded together, grubbing a scant mouthful now and again out of the woods, sniffing suspicion at your approach, ever on the alert to nab something and run? When he speaks of some perverse spirit as being perpetually "muley-hawed," has he not expressed the extreme of contrariness?

Terse and piquant proverbs abound in the everyday talk of mountain homes. If a man, in an attempt to put on too much Sunday style, comes to church carrying an umbrella, he is certain to be laughed at for "trying to hide the devil's leather from God's sun." If you do not

[176]

wish to accept an invitation to a meal, it is quite in order to answer, "No, thanks, I've jest drunk at the branch." If a boy boast that he has made something or some one run, it is sure to be suggested that he was "working in the lead." A sycophant is "anybody's dog that'll much him."

Here is a group of sayings all having reference to tale-bearing:

"There never was a hill so high but every old cow that went up it still carried her tail."

"A dog that will bring a bone will take one."

"In this district you can hear anything but ham a-fryin'."

Concerning poverty:

"A short horse is soon curried."

"When I get ready to move I jist shut the door and call the dogs and start."

"My land's so pore hit wouldn't raise a fight."

"Pore folks has a pore way, and rich folks has a mean one."

It has happened more than once in the history of the world that a collection of just such proverbs has formed the beginning of a literature.

[177]

And if songs and tales and rhymes that have never been rendered into letters can be said to be literature, we surely have one of our own, however crude it may be. There are no great poems in it, no passionate outpourings except those of religious feeling. The outlook is never higher than that of the genial and homely philosopher. But, while it rises to no grand heights, it is yet thoroughly healthful in tone; it meanders through all the sunny valleys of the mind, and has too keen a sense of the ridiculous ever to fall into a slough of despond.

Here is a tale, to begin with:

"Thar was a old widder-man with six childern lived in Jim county, and he married a Sequatchie widder that had six childern, too; and then they had six more. One day the whole passel of 'em got to fightin', and the old woman poked her head out o' the door and hollered to her man, 'Come hyer with a hick'ry, quick; your childern's a-whuppin' my childern, and they're all about to tromple the life out of our childern!'"

[178]

That is "a chestnut"—that is to say, a bit of standard fiction. There are hundreds of these. When a braggart begins to make too much of his prowess with a rifle, some one is likely to cap his tale with the long extravaganza about the Fortunate Hunter, whose Munchausen adventures end by his shooting a deer with a peach seed, and finding it afterwards grown into a tree on the deer's back, a burlesque that has no particular excuse for being outside of the mountaineer's innate enjoyment of absurd situations.

A large book might be compiled of disconnected quatrains and couplets that are fitted now into this song and now into that, as the singer pleases. A good collection of these stray fragments would, it seems to me, be worth the while of many a scholar. I shall have space here for but a few:

I.

Old Sam Simonses young Sam Simons is
  Old Sam Simonses son;
And young Sam Simons will be old Sam Simons
  When old Sam Simons is hung.

II.

If I had a scolding wife,
  Sure as you are born,
I'd take her down to Market Street
  And trade her off for corn.
For smoke in the house and a scolding wife
Leads a man a terrible life.

III.

There was an old man who had a wooden leg;
He hadn't no tobacco and he didn't want to beg;
He's got no tobacco for to chaw, chaw, chaw,
He's got no tobacco for to chaw!

IV.

I asked that gal to be my wife,
  And what do you reckon she said?
She said she wouldn't marry me
  If all the boys was dead!

Longer compositions are usually cast somewhat in the old ballad form. I select one:

THE ROVING SOLDIER.

When I was a rovin' soldier,
  I roved from town to town,
And wherever I saw a table set,
  There freely I sat down.

I hadn't been in Newark
  More than two days or three,
Till I fell in love with a pretty little gal
  And she in love with me.

She took me into her best room,
  She's given me a fan,
She's whispered low in her mother's ear,
  "I love the soldier man.

"I'll bundle up my calico,
  All ready for to go,
And roam this country over,
  Wherever he may go.

"And when you see us comin' back,
  You'll wring your hands for joy,

[181]

And one will say to another,
　'Yonder comes the soldier boy,

" 'With his pockets lined with greenbacks,
　His musket in his hand;
Hit's a long, long life and a full success
　To the Rovin' Soldier man.' "

These four songs are typical:

I.

I WENT UPON THE MOUNTAIN.

I went upon the mountain to see what I could
　hear,
　Lollee tru-dum tru-dum tru-dum lollee day;
I thought I heared my mother a-talkin' to my
　dear,
　Lollee tru-dum tru-dum tru-dum lollee day.

"I will not wash your dishes, I will not milk your
　cow,
　Lollee tru-dum tru-dum tru-dum lollee day;

[182]

For I'm a-gwine to marry—the fit has took me
    now,
  Lollee tru-dum," etc.

"Go 'long and wash your dishes, and stop your
    clatterin' tongue;
Talk about your marryin'! you're seven years
    too young.
"I'd like for you to tell me where you could git
    a man!"
"Oh, now, mammy, here is handsome Sam!"

II.

OLD DAN TUCKER.

Hi-yi-oh, for old Dan Tucker!
He's too late to come to his supper;
Supper's over and breakfast's a-cookin',
And old Dan Tucker's a-standin' a-lookin'.

Old Dan Tucker's a bad old man;
He whupped his wife with a fryin' pan;
He combed his head on the wagon-wheel,
And died with the toothache in his heel.

[183]

Old Dan Tucker he oncet got drunk,
Fell in the fire and kicked out a chunk;
Fire hit flew all in his shoe,
And away went old Dan Tucker, too.

III.

CRIPPLE CREEK.

Goin' up Cripple Creek, goin' in a run,
Goin' up Cripple Creek to have a little fun;
I roll my breeches to my knees,
And wade old Cripple Creek when I please.
Goin' up Cripple Creek, layin' in the shade,
Waitin' for the money that the old man made.

IV.

A FRAGMENT.

("The old sow measled, and she died last
spring.")
What ye gwine to do with the old sow's hide?
M-hm!
What ye gwine to do with the old sow's hide?
Make the best saddle that you ever did ride,
M-hm!
[184]

What ye gwine to do with the old sow's feet?
    M-hm!
What ye gwine to do with the old sow's feet?
Make the best souce that you ever did eat,
    M-hm!

What ye gwine to do when the meat gives out?
    M-hm!
What ye gwine to do when the meat gives out?
Set thar in the corner with your mouth stuck out,
    M-hm!

There is a good song about a young man who is seeking a wife. One girl promises to accept him if his corn crop is all that it should be, but—

"She went to the fence and she peep-ed in;
The grass and the weeds was up to her chin.
Said, 'A rake and a hoe and a fan-tail plow
Would do you better than a wife just now.' "

These two love-songs are the only ones of na-

tive composition that I have ever heard. They
are simple and tender as an old Scotch ballad:

I.

I've been gatherin' flowers in the meadow
　To wreathe around your head,
But so long you have kept me a-waitin',
　They're all withered and dead.

I've been gatherin' flowers on the hillside
　To bind them on your brow,
But so long you have kept me a-waitin',
　The flowers are faded now.

II.

O many a mile with you I've wandered,
　And many an hour with you I've spent,
Till I thought your heart was mine forever,
　But now I know hit was only lent.

Now I will seek some distant river,
　And there I'll spend my days and years;
I'll eat no food but the green willow,
　And drink no water but my tears.

[186]

There are some good ballads about the Civil War, and even a few that date back to the Revolution. But the real nuggets, to my thinking, are to be found among the children's rhymes. The list of these is inexhaustible, and even with Stevenson and J. Whitcomb Riley and Mother Goose to choose from, they are favorites in the log church school.

I.

I had a little rooster, and he crowed for day;
'Long come a fox and carried him away.

I had a little dog, and he was so true,
He showed me the place where the pigs went
   through.

I had a little sow, and fed her on slop,
And when we killed her we all had sop.

II.

Chicken pie, made of rye:
  A 'possum was the meat;
Rough enough, and tough enough,
  But more'n we all can eat.

[187]

III.

'Possum up a gum stump,
    Cooney in the holler;
Little boy, you shake 'em out,
    I'll give you half a dollar.

'Possum up a gum stump,
    Cooney in the holler,
And a little gal at pappy's house
    As fat as she can waller.

Our version of the Five Little Pigs—baby's
toes, of course—is really superior to that found
in Mother Goose since it tells a story, while the
Mother Goose version does not:

This little pig says, "Let's steal some wheat."
This little pig says, "Where'll ye git it at?"
This little pig says, "In master's barn."
This little pig says, "I'll run and tell."
This little pig says, "Quee, quee, quee, can't get
    over the door-sill!"

[188]

Inasmuch as it contains the American spirit, humorous and honest, this literature of a humble folk may contribute toward the formation of that national literature which the American people are seeking. Let no one who would welcome an expression truly national despise the quaint lore of the Southern mountaineers. We have had no Robert Burns as yet; but I expect him.

CHAPTER X

CONCLUSION

"What is to be will be, and that that ain't to be
might happen."

M Y people, everywhere on the borders of
the mountain country, are being laid
hold of and swept away by the oncoming tide of
civilization, that drowns as many as it uplifts.
And in this way:

One day a hotel is built, a summer settlement
begun, in some fastness of the mountains hith-
erto secluded from the outer world. The pure
air, the mineral waters, are advertised abroad,
and the summer people begin to come in. Good
roads are built in place of the old creek-beds and
trails, and rubber-tired carriages whirl past the
plodding oxen and mule teams. Handsome cottages are erected in contrast to the cabins, and
sunbonnets turn aside in wonder at bright crea-
tions of roses and chiffon. The mountain people

come in groups to look on, some from homes so deep in the woods that the children take fright at the approach of even a home-made "tar-grinder" wagon. They are easily bewildered, of course, and cannot at once respond to the need of a new standard of values. Perhaps instead of a hotel it is a factory or a mill of some kind that presents the thin edge of the wedge, but the results are as certain to follow.

When the cottages are occupied the trouble begins. The hotel may bring its own servants; but for the summer people there are washing and sewing to be done by the women, and work in gardens and stables by the men of the place. Later, they are hired as house servants, and as caretakers during the winter season, when the houses must stand empty. All this is hardly to be avoided, perhaps, but a host of evils follow. Here is an easy way of making money, and the old pursuits are abandoned. Men neglect their farms and the fashioning of sturdy home-made implements and utensils. It is easier, far, to buy city tools with city money. Their teams are con-

[191]

stantly in demand for hauling, moving households up in the spring and down in the fall. They have never worked so hard before, nor been so well paid. The strenuous life has laid hold of them. It seems for a time that better days have dawned for the half-starved and the ignorant among us.

Is it any wonder that false ambitions creep in? The lady of the hotel or cottage, when she packs her trunks to go home, leaves sundry trinkets out for the mountain girl who has served her— half-worn clothing such as the poor child has never seen before, trimmed hats, books and magazines, if she can read. The recipient plans for a similar donation next year. She does not willingly return to sunbonnet and homespun. Her old mother cares little for the new clothes, but sees at once how much easier it is to buy blankets than to spin and weave. So the loom and wheel are consigned to the barn loft, where they fall to pieces with dry-rot, and the woman forgets her coverlet patterns. The hand of the worker in wood and metal loses its cunning. The grow-

[192]

ing lads scarcely learn to shoe a horse; they are all too busy working for the city people.

The value of money, the false importance of riches, is evident to their minds before the need of education. They become avaricious, they who were wont to share their last chew of tobacco, and put the children to earning, by picking berries or what not, instead of sending them to school. For by this time the city people have helped to build a schoolhouse in the district. The old-time hospitality is crowded out of existence, and under the influence of women, who imagine that a man who does not know when to take off his hat cannot possibly be courteous, the fine old manners disappear. The old music is supplanted by cheap Sunday-school song-books, that contain shaped notes and directions so clear that the wayfaring man who has learned to sing on the do-re-mi-fa-sol basis, though he knows not one key from another, need not err therein. The homespuns, with their delightful dull colors of root and bark, are ousted by aniline-dyed calicoes which do not wear more than a season. The

[193]

beauty of simple smoke-browned interiors is blotted out with newspapers pasted, coat upon coat, on the walls for additional warmth, since paper is easier come by than substantial chinking. Drugged barrel-house liquor takes the place of the clear, fiery product of the still, making the evil of drunkenness ten times worse. The old dances are given over to rowdies. A new standard of morals is set up amid the confusion. Even the old religion is passing, laughed away by empty-headed ones who never could understand a thing so sacred. This people who have no servant class are constantly made to feel themselves inferior to the newcomers, and so fall into servility. The old dignity has slipped from them before they are aware, and they grasp but vainly after that alien possession, an education, which they are told would establish them in the new.

At last some, more thoughtful than the rest, awake to the fact that they are growing old in a service which provides no pension, growing old without the support of the well-tended acres

[194]

that were their forefathers' mainstay. Too late the mountaineer realizes that he has sold his birthright for a mess of pottage. He has become a day laborer, with nothing better in store, and can give his sons no heritage but the prospect of working by the day. If he is wise he counsels them against entering on the treadmill of one-dollar-a-day that has used up his best years' strength. But some follow the line of least resistance unheeding, and many more are handicapped from the start by their elders' mistake, so that only a few are able to take advantage of the new environment far enough to obtain an education or learn a trade.

"Have we not built roads for a people too lazy to build for themselves?" say the city people. "Have we not served them in many ways? Are not church, school and newspaper a true benefit, a light in their ignorance?"

In short, *haven't we paid them well?*

They do not understand that the semblance of prosperity is only a temporary illusion that vanishes with the departure of the summer peo-

[195]

ple. With the first frost a change is felt, and the new conditions are found to be anything but a blessing. If the old-time mountaineer never knew the taste of ice-cream in summer, he was, on the other hand, never without corn-pones and side-meat in cold weather. If his "old woman" never had a hat trimmed with silk, she had homespun petticoats and stockings instead. There are now no more hog-killings on the old scale that filled the smokehouses to overflowing every fall. The wives and mothers have no such quilts and blankets as they used to keep folded away. They have been too busy making money all summer to prepare against the breath of the north. Now the money is gone who-knows-where, and if the summer people could see these poor folk huddled round their fires in cheap store calicoes which have to be renewed every two or three months—see them buying meal by the half-peck to eat with the invariable white gravy, they would not think the pay so well proportioned to the sacrifice, after all.

Some there are who refuse to be drawn into

the whirlpool. One such lad cried to his brother, who was hired for the season to a city man: "Jim, I wouldn't take the talk that fellow gives you for double your wages, for anything."

"You'll have to learn to take a good many things, if you want to make any money," answered the brother; but he spoke with a shamed face, for he still smarted from a quarrel with his employer.

"Right thar ye deny your raisin', Jim," said the boy, sadly. "You've went so long without seein' money that you're plumb mesmerized if anybody shakes a dollar bill in front of ye!"

May the day be far distant when the Log Church neighborhood shall be overtaken by this fate! I have heard it said that civilization, when it touches the people of the backwoods, acts as a useful precipitant in thus sending the dregs to the bottom. As a matter of fact, it is only the shrewder and more determined, not the truly fit, that survive in this struggle. Among these very submerged ones, reduced to dependence on an alien people, there are thousands who inherit the skill of their forefathers who fashioned their own locks, musical instruments and guns. And these very women who are breaking health and spirit over a thankless tub of suds ought surely to turn their talents to better account, ought to be designing and weaving coverlets and Roman-striped rugs, or "piecing" the quilt patterns now so popular.

Need these razors be used to cut grindstones? Must this free folk who are in many ways the truest Americans of America be brought under the yoke of caste division, to the degradation of all their finer qualities, merely for lack of the right work to do?

Let it be made clear that here is no question of "elevating the masses" in the ordinary sense of the term. That task awaits the world everywhere. In the mountains the need is for development not foreign to our natures, cultivation of talents already in blossom. Let us be given work that will make us better mountaineers, instead of turning us into poor imitation city people.

[198]

In my desire that the mountaineers shall be developed along the line of their peculiar talents I am not alone. Over and again experiment has proved that wherever it is possible for them to live by their own handiwork they are as self-respecting, honest and enterprising a people as any that America can boast. And even while educating themselves and their children, at a cost of effort and sacrifice that makes their unselfishness deserve the name of heroism, they will yet preserve the old simplicity, the old customs, and even the dialect among themselves. Several such settlements have been established already, where the industries encouraged are those crafts in which the mountaineers excel—weaving, woodwork, basket-making and quilting; where there is no talk of master and servant, and the old type is preserved. May one and another take up the thread until it shall be woven into the rich fabric of national life and thought.

I make the statement more as a hope than as a prophecy, but I feel sure of my ground in saying that these North American Highlanders will

[199]

yet become a grand race; a race that shall stand for freedom political and industrial; a race that can no more endure unjust rule than it can thrive in the tainted air of the low country. Types come and pass in nature's scheme of economy, but not until their usefulness is ended. The mountaineers are a young people, not ready to pass away; their strength lies dormant, awaiting its hour. To the mountains, in time to come, we may look for great men, thinkers as well as workers, leaders of religious and poetic thought, and statesmen above all. So much passionate loyalty cannot be lost to the Government, must find expression in redeemers of practical politics as well as in military service. From the mountains will yet arise a quickening of American ideals and American life.

But before such renaissance the mountaineers must awaken to consciousness of themselves as a people. For although throughout the highlands of Kentucky, Tennessee and the Carolinas our nature is one, our hopes, our loves, our daily life the same, we are yet a people asleep, a race without knowledge of its own existence. This condition is due, as I have tried to show in the chapter called "Neighbors," to the isolation that separates the mountaineer from all the world but his own blood and kin, and to the consequent utter simplicity of social relations. When they shall have established a unity of thought corresponding to their homogeneity of character, then their love of country will assume a practical form, and then, indeed, America, with all her peoples, can boast no stronger sons than these same mountaineers.

Looking upon the fresh, sweet young faces of the children of the Log Church school, I often wonder which of them is destined to carry forth the word to his people for a Gathering of the Clans, not to war, but to work—work that shall uplift instead of degrading; work that shall make the influence of the mountaineers a peculiar and beneficent force in their beloved country and in the world of men.

THE END

INDEX TO THE NEW EDITION

THE UNIVERSITY OF
TENNESSEE PRESS
KNOXVILLE